SPECTACLE, REALITY

Confronting a culture of militarism

David Gee

ForcesWatch

David Gee has written and campaigned extensively on the ethics of military recruitment and the mental health of veterans. His first book, *Holding Faith: Creating peace in a violent world*, explored nonviolence and social change. He is a co-founder of ForcesWatch.

ForcesWatch critically scrutinises the ethics of armed forces recruitment practices and challenges efforts to embed militarist values in civilian society.

For more information see www.forceswatch.net.

Published in 2014 by ForcesWatch
5 Caledonian Road, London N1 9DY
www.forceswatch.net

ISBN: 978 0 9930955 0 4

Cover image: 'The View from the Drone; Northern Pakistan (23 January 2009)' by Steve Pratt, 200cm x 200cm, oil and acrylic on canvas.

Printed by Russell Press

Contents

INTRODUCTION

In 2014, the Royal Mint announced that the first of four new designs for £2 coins to mark the First World War centenary would be Kitchener's famous icon. We all know the image: the imposing, moustachioed stare of a war hero demanding that the country's young men ennoble themselves in another patriotic war because 'Your country needs you.'

That noble war never took place. Years of slaughter left 20 million people dead and as many again seriously injured in the most cataclysmic episode of violence the world had seen. At the time Kitchener's portrait was bearing down on the youth of Britain no one foresaw how appalling the suffering would be, but even had the war been shorter it would have sent young men to ignoble, violent deaths as all wars do. It would still have mobilised working people to fight at the behest of their ruling class. And it would still have wracked the course of history with resentment, guilt, and the next war.

The noble war fantasy is the first of the poster's deceits. A second is the figure it portrays. When Britain's young people a century ago saw him, they did not see Kitchener the man, but Kitchener the legend. Field Marshal Earl Herbert Horatio Kitchener of Broome and Khartoum KG, KP, GCB, OM, GCSI, GCMG, GCIE, ADC, PC, grandee of the Empire and warrior hero, back from crushing successive popular rebellions in colonial Africa, symbolised the indomitable British spirit. The grizzled patriot would surely inspire men to enlist, so the government had made him Secretary of War.

Next to Kitchener the legend, the unvarnished reality of Kitchener the man had been all but strained out of the public imagination. His forces achieved their most notable victory, at Omdurman in the Sudan in 1898, by simple dint of the superior firepower of the world's dominant empire. A few machine guns, which had only recently been invented, were placed before 50,000 Sudanese soldiers armed with swords and muskets. Half a million bullets later, nearly 11,000 of them were dead and as many again injured. Kitchener had the enemy's groaning wounded executed the same day.[1] He would later raze the tomb of the rebels' spiritual leader, their 'Mahdi', keeping the skull for a trophy and throwing the bones in the Nile.[2]

Kitchener's legend suggested nothing of this to the young minds of 1914. His image is an icon made from reality, but whose history has been scooped out to leave a hollow symbol of imperial patriotism. Kitchener the man is just a man. Kitchener the symbol is a figment of propaganda intended to convince us of something we would not otherwise believe. In effect, the poster goes to work on us by employing one deceit – Kitchener's legend – to invoke another – a fantasy of virtuous violence. When the war's madness had ended, the public rued the cheap pretensions of the early war propaganda, which is why we ought to be wary now of its use on the back of a coin.

In pushing from view the real Kitchener and the real nature of warfare, the propagandists who devised the poster lied twice, but to swing Britons roundly behind the war, a third sleight was also necessary. The war was born not of a quarrel between the peoples of Europe, but between their rulers, who in each case had imperial interests to preserve. The German factory worker had no grudge to bear against his counterpart in Britain or France unless his government could beguile him otherwise with the rhetoric of patriotic militarism. Similarly in Britain, to initiate war was the state's choice, not the people's, yet the war itself would depend entirely on the well-corralled, body-and-mind compliance of the working masses. What better way to achieve this than to tell the public that this was their war, fought for their sake, and that they were needed? The propagandists of France, Germany, Russia and Austria-Hungary did the same, in each case largely convincing their public that they needed the war to take place. All warring states do the same today.

The Royal Mint now uncritically reproduces the wartime propaganda image millions of times over on its new coin in order, it says, to educate the public about the start of the First World War.

In choosing the design, the Mint admitted that they were more interested in the symbol than the man,[3] yet as a symbol the portrait does not stand for the war that took place, but for a romantic spectacle of war distanced from the realities of history.

The Kitchener image is an emblem of a militarist culture, namely one that relies heavily on military action, values, and worldviews for its national identity and its foreign policy. Such a culture of militarism is part of our way of life as a society. A militarist outlook is embedded in certain perceptions of British nationhood and its security, in political orientations and the policies that come from them, in our fears and hopes for the future, in the language we use and stories we tell about the way the world works, and in our entertainment, arts, and media productions.

Whereas culture of a given character is held in the objects we make, such as the Kitchener poster, it is perpetuated and propagated by the people who believe in it or are willing to go along with it. In Britain, a culture of militarism might be said to rest on the values, worldviews and behaviours of three overlapping groups of people. A first group, but not the largest, is people for whom a militarist worldview reflects a considered belief about how best to keep the nation and its people safe. The logical conclusion of that view is a heavily militarised world, which is hardly a recipe for security, but the conviction is an honest one. For a second group, the value of militarism lies in furthering agendas that have little or nothing to do directly with security. For example, militarism is fostered by those who want the United States to take Britain seriously as a strategic partner, or who worry that the public might not support Britain's future wars in far-away places, or whose business is to make arms here and sell them abroad. Those who are nostalgic for Britain's imperial status, or whose patriotic sense of national identity feels inconceivable without the assumed heroism of Britain's soldiery, are also in this group of ideological militarists. This group commonly justify their views in terms of prudent national security while their primary motives lie elsewhere.

The 'honest militarists' and the 'ideological militarists' are few when compared with a third group, whom we could call the 'casual militarists'. For these, questions of war and security are marginal. They are perhaps wary of encouraging their children to join the forces, but happy to wave a flag for 'our heroes' at a military parade. As this book will discuss, government initiatives like Armed Forces Day and school cadet forces are largely aimed at shoring up and extending this group, which is wont to accept militarism relatively uncritically as natural and laudable in our national culture.

Just as certain groups in society hold a militarist outlook, so militarism also shapes society's perceptions of war and security. Kitchener's propaganda image, for example, achieves three socio-cultural functions of militarism: it distances the public from the disturbing realities of warfare; it imagines war romantically as a glorious quest; and it attempts to control public actions, values, and worldviews by aligning them with its own. This book explores these dynamics in turn – distance, romance, control – in three essays that may be read separately or together. Accompanying these are three short, stand-alone, story-like pieces about the cultural treatment of war and resistance to it. All the book's sections explore the themes of its title: war as spectacle, war as reality, and resistance to war and militarism.

I hope this book will help to spur on a conversation in society about the effects of war on the world and of militarism on our social culture. That conversation is needed, whatever one's views may be. I will be clear about my own. My standpoint is one of deep scepticism about the value of armed force, and abhorrence of its effects on combatants, civilian bystanders, relations between peoples, and the integrity of the earth. I am equally sceptical of the heroic narratives frequently used to frame and justify the abject violence of war. Nonetheless, while preparing the text I have been keenly aware that I too am telling only one possible story, which has weaknesses and limitations like any other. I have not voiced many of these 'ifs and buts' in these pages, preferring to leave other stories for others to tell.

Throughout, I have sought to give weight to both the cultural successes of militarism and its failures. The ideological defeats of war propaganda are due in no small part to active resistance by social movements and, I think, a healthy public scepticism of state justifications for contemporary wars. In this respect, I am surprised to have finished the work feeling more hopeful than when I started. I hope that you will feel the same.

DISTANCE

On one night in 1945, more than a thousand British and American bombers turned some 11 square miles of central Dresden to ash and rubble. The policy of targeting the central residential areas of German cities meant that the dead were almost all civilians, numbering in the tens of thousands. Most died by burning or asphyxiation in the firestorm.

First to arrive above the city that night was, as usual, the RAF master bomber in his Mosquito. His job was to circle low over the target area, monitor the bombers' accuracy, and send corrective directions as necessary. The sky was clear and the city undefended, so almost all the bombs landed right on target, generating the intended uncontrollable fire. The RAF radio communications are preserved in a wire recording. 'Good bombing... nice bombing', reported the master bomber to the Lancasters as they turned for home.[4]

How does the brutal killing of tens of thousands of ordinary people and their children come to be 'nice'? Certainly, within the narrow terms of the bomber crews' role, their raid had been successful; the master bomber was only pointing this out. Yet their role that night was mass murder. Perhaps the bomber crews were abstractly aware that they were burning and suffocating people to death, but their ready compliance with their orders suggests that few were viscerally disturbed by their actions at the time.[5]

While the bombers were turning for home, Margret Freyer, aged 24, was desperately trying to escape the firestorm below. She recalls being badly burned and stumbling through the intense heat between bouts of unconsciousness brought on by asphyxiation and exhaustion. Later, she recalled the scene at length to the historian Alexander McKee.

> 'From some of the debris poked arms, heads, legs, shattered skulls. The static water-tanks were filled up to the top with dead human beings, with large pieces of

masonry lying on top of that again. Most people looked as if they had been inflated, with large yellow and brown stains on their bodies. People whose clothes were still glowing… I think I was incapable of absorbing the meaning of this cruelty any more, for there were also so many little babies, terribly mutilated…'[6]

The failure of the Dresden bomber crews to know, in their feeling selves, the horrific consequences of their actions does not reveal a peculiar moral depravity on their part; they were not sociopaths, nor were they alone in the act's commission. Back home, politicians, the media, the Church, and the general public cheered the bombing on, despite knowing that it aimed to raze the residential heart of each city targeted. Opposition was scant and shouted down as unpatriotic.

The Dresden atrocity, as well as that at Cologne, Coventry, Hamburg and London before it, and Hiroshima and Nagasaki afterwards, arraign the moral imagination of entire societies. Ordinary people in Britain lent the bombings their moral support, despite being aware – abstractly, at least – of its effect on German people just as ordinary as themselves. Politicians and military commanders went further still, relishing the mass-destructive effect of their policy.[7] Would they have done so had they recognised it, as feeling human beings, for the brutality it was? Then, surely, even the staunchest advocates of the strategic value of the bombing would also have been the most conscientiously torn. They would have known, not only in their heads, but in their hearts also, that their policy was murdering people, including many children, on a massive scale.

Distance and moral imagination

As soldiers testify, close proximity to extreme violence is deeply disturbing to the psyche, which is why ordering them to kill at close quarters typically results in enduring stress and feelings of shame.[8] Research into the neuropsychology of empathy shows that when a person directly witnesses another's suffering, the pain centres of the observer's brain are activated.[9] Yet a little physical distance from the victims of violence – a few hundred feet in the Dresden master bomber's case – can prevent this reaction. We can be aware of deep suffering occurring just out of sight and not feel more than the slightest ruffle of discomfort. When evaluated morally, killing a hundred innocent people from a Lancaster bomber is no different from shooting them on the ground with a rifle, one by one. Experientially, however, one act is disquieting even to imagine; the other is easily committed without scruple, over and over again.

The philosopher David Hume noticed that it was not only possible, but commonplace, to be left unmoved by distant suffering.[10] Commonplace, but morally inadequate, he believed; there exists no strictly moral reason to care more about a violated stranger standing next to us than one on the other side of the world – as persons they are equally worthy of moral attention. For consistency, we ought to care about the fate of neither, which is sociopathic, or both, which is conscientious. In order to achieve this conscientious response, Hume suggested that we imagine witnessing distant suffering as if we were standing next to it and only then evaluate the situation morally. Applied to the Dresden raid, we would have to imagine accompanying Margret Freyer and the tens of thousands who perished in the firestorm, and then weigh the value of the bombing. That no imagination could ever encompass such overwhelming violence betrays the shocking brutality of the policy.

Hume's insight shows that moral evaluations rely on more than a chance feeling for others' wellbeing; they demand cognitive and emotional labour – reason, feeling, and imagination. Under this discipline it becomes possible to bring our fantasy of war closer to its reality – sufficiently close to become wary of facile forms of militarism that casually promote warfare. The consequence of failing to do this, and still more of not bothering, is that we become reduced as human beings – less than thoughtful, less than humane, and more willing to join in with the jingo. Simply put, we ought to know what war is, at the very least, before deciding whether or not to lend it support. When war is imagined unthinkingly, it thrives.

By trying to appreciate war events from the standpoints of those affected, we also draw closer to appreciating the equality that they share with us as human beings. Indeed, one way of understanding war is as the violent enactment of our mutual estrangement from one another, in which the psychic distance between the agents of violence and its victims remains unbridged. The deeper our estrangement from distant others – which is as much a form of estrangement from ourselves as from them – the greater the scale of the possible violation becomes. In other words, the further back we stand, the more harm we can do with impunity. This is why war by modern technology is so utterly destructive and, morally speaking, so dangerously easy to wage. Conversely, the stronger our empathic experience of our human neighbour, the harder it becomes to support his or her violation, still less to take part in it.

Hence, a culture of militarism depends on our being poor witnesses to war. Were we to try to appreciate war in the manner of a disciplined witness, we would come to recognise it as an industrial business by which people's bodies are punctured, torn, crushed, burned or otherwise mutilated on a mass scale. We would see that this is achieved principally by means of other people's bodies, aided by technology whose purpose is to magnify the efficiency of harm. 'Injury… is the relentless object of all military activity,'[11] writes Elaine Scarry, and 'the central goal in war is to out-injure the opponent'.[12] Beyond the violation of individuals at the epicentre of the violence, we would watch its shock-wave radiate outwards, ravaging families, communities, societies, cultures, economies, and the natural ecology by which people live. In such degrees of desolation, we might sense that the very dignity of our humanity is wounded, as if we shared as human beings a common soul that war offends, injures and reduces.

We would recognise that throughout the modern era, our societies have prized war as a righteous, redemptive act. They have committed great resource to war preparations and drawn their children's generation into the performance as the primary enactors of its violence. We would see, too, how the mass violence of war has taken varied shapes, from brief conflagrations to entrenched wars with drawn-out crescendos of mass violence. We would surely appreciate, too, that the violence of militarism is not always a form of war in the usual sense of the word. The people of occupied lands experience imperial military might as a presence lingering in the shadows, ready to crush the least smattering of dissent with overwhelming violence. To the occupying powers, such enforced quietude is experienced as a form of 'peace' – *Pax Romana*, *Pax Britannica*, and now the economic colonialism of *Pax Americana* – but the colonised know it for the violence it is. And we would also see that whilst war issues from the decisions of powerful men, its genesis lies more fully in cultures and systems of militarism, economies of oppression, and the vanities of the ruling class that have persisted through history.

A society sensitised to the horrific realities of war would surely be deeply disturbed by its persistent repetition and by the prospect of the pattern continuing to scar future generations. As ordinary citizens, we would certainly wonder at our own complicity in militarism and the wars it produces. At the least, we would share a distaste for war's glorification, a scepticism of our culture's casual affirmations of militarism, and a commitment to learning the ways of a just and sustainable peace. To borrow Margret Freyer's words, how many 'little babies, terribly mutilated' does it take for any goal, however valuable, to be worth war no longer? The only humane answer, surely, is 'one'.

The war spectacle

Most of us living in this island realm on the fringe of Europe encounter war from a safe distance – that is, in our imagination alone – and can afford to do so casually. Our experiential remoteness from the shocking realities of war allows a more convenient narrative to displace the pathos and discomfiture that war properly evokes in us as humane human beings. From such a casual, distant perspective, soldiers are universally promoted to 'heroes', as if the cardinal virtue of their profession were heroic choice rather than obedience to orders. If a roadside bomb blows a soldier into pieces, he has 'made the ultimate sacrifice', as if he had chosen his own death, and his ignominiously eviscerated body joins 'our glorious dead'. A soldier on the other side of the war is never heroic, always 'the enemy', always nameless, and not killed but 'neutralised'. Nor does he number among 'the fallen', which is another euphemism reserved exclusively for our own; if the enemy dies it is because 'the target will fall when hit' and his demise becomes our trophy. If war kills, maims, or bereaves civilians, or denies them their livelihoods, they become 'collateral damage', a regrettable secondary product of the violence, despite civilians' corpses being, in fact, the primary physical product of all war in the last century.

This is conveniently distancing language. It is genteel, fanciful, showy in its solemnity. Its lofty pretensions consign the flesh and guts of war to the margins, preferring instead disembodied euphemism in which persons in their diversity – with hopes, fears, families, loves, and life stories – are replaced by ghostly, depersonalised, dehumanised figments: heroes, enemies, collateral. In sum, the language lies.

The images that this narrative of nobility mobilises are equally euphemistic. The logo of the most popular armed forces charity, Help for Heroes, depicts a silhouetted wounded soldier being carried to safety on a stretcher. Like all the soldiers represented in the publicity of this and other major veterans' charities, this stylised exemplar is not crying out in pain, does not have permanent brain damage, is not trying to stop his own guts from spilling out. Lest we be in any doubt, the patient gives us the thumbs-up to reassure us that all will end well. In effect, the image conceptually contains the warfare within a narrative of recovery, salving away the trauma and quenching the critical question of whether the war should be taking place. The logo tells us what we want to hear: our war is heroic and its harm can be healed. Only a short step from this is the notion that violence is reversible, and that warfare is not anathema to civilisation but a natural part of it.

The language and symbols of the noble war are embedded in culture through public ritual. Perhaps most notable among these is the British Legion's annual poppy appeal and Remembrance Festival, as it is now known. In the past, public commemoration of Britain's wars has included shades of pride and lament, gratitude and repentance, but despite this ambivalence, quiet thoughtfulness has commonly and appropriately marked our remembrance. In recent years, the British Legion has turned the commemoration into a sprawling, jingoistic jamboree, exploiting its huge fundraising potential using all the tricks of the charity trade. The organisation commodifies remembrance as vanity trinkets with its range of poppy jewellery, turns it into a flutter with its Poppy Lottery worth £2,000 each week, and capitalises on the public's fetish for fame by auctioning off celebrities' poppy-branded clothing. Girl band The Saturdays were commissioned to launch the poppy appeal in 2013 with their innuendo-strewn song, *Notorious*: 'I've been a bad girl / I'm a bad girl / I'm notorious'; a cloud of poppies fell from the ceiling while the crowd cheered.

The poppy itself used to be worn one or two days before Remembrance Sunday; it now fills the streets for a fortnight. All public figures are expected to wear one. TV presenters are even made to wear one;[13] if TV guests are not wearing one when they arrive, they are given one.[14] Given the poppy's popularity, we ought to have a shared understanding of its meaning, but it has always been ambiguous. After the First World War, a committed sentiment of 'Never Again' percolated through the population, which coloured the meaning of the poppy when it was first introduced. Today, poppies are sold on railway stations by current forces personnel calling, 'Support the troops?' Surely the poppy cannot carry both meanings without contradiction.

The British Legion, which owns the rights to the poppy as a trade mark,[15] does not say what it is meant to help us remember, but the annual remembrance parade in London perhaps provides a hint. That ceremony invites us to lionise British and commonwealth fatalities as 'The Glorious Dead', as inscribed on the Cenotaph in Whitehall, but not formally to remember civilians or enemy combatants who suffered in war. The ceremony, which brings the armed forces together with politicians, royals and the Church, is framed as a moment of searching reflection, but the institution of war itself escapes critical scrutiny. Most people who wear a poppy do so in good faith, but as the official ceremony's emblem it now appears to be another symbol of selective amnesia. The white poppy, which is offered as an alternative emblem of remembrance, has a clearer meaning. According to the Peace Pledge Union which makes them, they signify remembrance of all the victims of wars – whether soldiers or civilians, whether 'ours' or 'theirs' – and declare a commitment to build a culture of peace.[16]

Rather than challenging us to remember war, the Remembrance Festival, aided by the poppy appeal, wraps our collective historical memory in a glitzy veil. Doubts about the legitimacy of war itself, which properly belong to remembrance as an act of moral imagination, are nowhere to be found. With the collusion of the media and public, and with financial support from corporations including the major arms dealer BAE Systems,[17] the remembrance period is now a festival of forgetting. Meanwhile, the British Legion exploits its position as the self-appointed National Custodian of Remembrance to perform its alchemy, turning our genuine desire for collective commemoration into gold; it is now a corporate-style charity-business with an annual income of around £130 million. The Legion, Help for Heroes, and other major veterans' charities do valuable work, but now make so much money that the state can devolve to them a large share of its practical responsibility for the men and women it sent to war.

If the Legion's Remembrance Festival lends social licence to British militarism, the Church is mobilised to provide divine sanctification. While many ordinary Christians are involved in peace and anti-war witness inspired by their faith, corporately the Church has historically blessed Britain's wars. The Church of England held substantial shares in arms companies until a long campaign finally persuaded its reluctant leadership in 2000 to put its money somewhere else.[18] Senior clergy have even blessed Britain's Trident nuclear programme, apparently willing to overlook that the payload of just one submarine is capable of repeating the horrors of Dresden in 40 cities in just a few minutes.

It would be awkward for the main churches to stand against British wars when they are institutionally embedded in the armed forces through their military chaplains. Although they tend to claim neutrality with respect to war, chaplains are unavoidably compromised by their service to two masters. On the one hand, they serve the state and are enrolled into the worldview of the armed forces. On the other, they are called to serve their God, who marks the fall of every sparrow and whose prophets foretell an end to war.[19] Army chaplains' motto, *In this sign, conquer*, unambiguously indicates their salient purpose as sanctifiers of armed violence. The phrase is taken from Constantine's vision on the eve of battle that he would win if his forces marked their weapons and shields with the Cross.

The same symbolic sanctification of war becomes ritualised in military church services that give thanks for victory and grieve for dead comrades but do not, as Falklands veteran Ken Lukowiak noted, beg forgiveness as humankind for the shameful carnage.[20] These services offer comfort, as faith should, but fall shy of another responsibility of their ministry, namely to voice the discomfiting questions provoked by the abject violence of war.

Many Christians have been flummoxed and dismayed by what they see as their institutions' failure to break ranks from the state and resist its wars, although Scottish churches and the Bishops in Wales are the notable general exception, often having criticised aspects of state militarism.[21] There are some outspoken critics in the Church of England, too. In 2007, Stephen Cottrell, then Bishop of Reading, held a service on the road outside the Trident base at Faslane, Scotland, where he made his own view clear: 'Nuclear weapons are an affront to God. Therefore, I am happy to join you in making a little trouble for peace.'[22] Today, a good number of Christians still travel to Faslane to join the protests and make their own creative trouble. A number of clergy began by supporting war as Christ's work, only to repent later. George Zabelka, the US Air Force chaplain who blessed the nuclear attacks against Japan in 1945, was plunged into crisis after he visited the devastated city of Nagasaki.[23] He later worked in the civil rights movement with Martin Luther King, whose commitment to nonviolence inspired the former military chaplain to a fresh conviction about the Church's proper witness in relation to war:

'There is no way to follow Christ, to love as Christ loved, and simultaneously to kill other people. It is a lie to say that the spirit that moves the trigger of a flamethrower is the Holy Spirit. It is a lie to say that learning to kill is learning to be Christ-like. It is a lie to say that learning to drive a bayonet into the heart of another is motivated from having put on the mind of Christ. Militarized Christianity is a lie. It is radically out of conformity with the teaching, life, and spirit of Jesus.'[24]

Using a similar line of reasoning, but framed in secular terms, one of the peace activists' arguments is that weapons of mass destruction and similar structures of violence count against the quality of our humanity and our civilisation. The argument is immediately persuasive for most of us, I suspect, but remains an outsider perspective in a society whose values and worldviews are shaped by a culture of militarism. The government, mainstream press, most of the political establishment, impresarios of popular culture, senior officers in the armed forces, and even major veterans' charities use their formidable cultural capital to shape a social milieu in which the terror and horror of war are marginalised in awareness.

The process of shaping public consciousness for militarism begins with children in their early years. The Israeli peace activist Sahar Vardi remembers learning how to count by matching the numbers from 1 to 10 with clusters of stylised tanks, fighter jets and other military hardware, for example.[25] This does not turn children into militarists, but it does impress upon them – at around four years of age – that killing machines belong in the world in the same way as the apples, bananas and carrots of the ABC.

The inculcation of militarist values and worldviews continues through childhood, particularly through play. While the young have always fantasised fighting – Roman children played with wooden swords, for example – the ascendency of militarised play in the modern era began with the early stages of mass production in the late 19th Century, when cast-lead soldiers eclipsed the train set as the most popular toy for British children.[26] Before his quasi-pacifist years, H G Wells wryly hoped that this would help 'the British Empire [to] gain new strength from nursery floors'.[27] After the First World War, with memories of senseless carnage still fresh, the popularity of war play fell away, but then bounced back. In the wake of the nuclear attacks on Japan, an American toy firm designed a small, wooden, glass-topped box, a few inches square, containing two ball-bearings stuffed into pill capsules to resemble bombs. The child's objective was to roll these into holes labelled 'Hiroshima' and 'Nagasaki' on a map of Japan printed on the bottom of the container.[28] When the Cold War arms race was gathering pace, more toys were developed to imitate nuclear war. One such gadget was a spring-loaded nuclear missile with USAF branding and packed with caps to simulate a detonation.[29] How excited the child must have been when told that their state possessed thousands of these, albeit much larger, and that the fantasised target had a real-world name: Russia.

Older children can upgrade their war play at local cadet forces. In Britain, children have been able to join the cadets since the 1850s, when schoolboys were mobilised to supplement the armed forces as child soldiers to repel a possible French invasion. George Orwell recalled that at the age of seven, just before the First World War, he 'was a member of the Navy League and wore a sailor suit with "HMS Invincible" on my cap'.[30] Swept up in what he called the middle classes' moral training for war, he started handling a rifle from the age of 10 and continued to do so through public school cadet corps and then the Officer Training Corps. Today, the cadets are a major soft recruitment tool and serve as an initial training programme for those still too young to enlist. Dressed in combat fatigues, faces camouflaged, and armed with real rifles loaded with blanks, boys and girls from age 12 are taught to advance on an enemy position in the manner of a real infantry platoon. Abstracted from killing and the fear of being killed, the cadet's experience is still just a fantasy, but it feels real and is all the more exciting for it.

The language and symbolism of noble warfare, its ritualisation and sanctification through public events, and the acculturation process through childhood and adolescence, go some way to indicating why we are apt to shrink from appreciating war for the horror that it is. As I hope to show in this book, we still harbour a healthy scepticism of militarism and its wars, as evidenced by the huge march of 15 February 2003 and other instances of mass public protest. Even so, in degrees we prefer the moral soporific of a more manageable, culturally acceptable story to one that stirs our deeper humanity and provokes us into resistance.

We are thus primed to receive news of war less critically than we might. Given that relatively few of us hear direct, unedited testimony from the people affected by warfare, we rely heavily on mass media to tell it like it is. The tacit promise of the media is that they enable us to follow the real events of warfare as they take place, but media organisations can just as easily push the realities of warfare to the margins as bring them to awareness.

The public only became able to follow the events of distant warfare in the 19th Century, when nascent global communications allowed newspapers to report events on the ground with a time-lag of just a few days. The cultural historian Graham Dawson describes in detail how, in 1857, the press whipped up and fed the public's lascivious appetite for violence against mutineering native Indian soldiers under command of the East India Company.[31] As General Havelock's 'flying column' crossed the subcontinent to quell the uprising and staunch Indians' emerging hopes of independence, the papers presented his journey as a series of derring-do adventures. The public could feel they were vicariously witnessing a righteous war, but in reality it was a bloody mess of confusion and privation, with horrific acts of brutality by both sides. When the Indian mutiny was eventually crushed, *Lloyds Weekly* reported the story's conclusion just as its readers would have liked to believe it really was, despite Havelock's inconvenient death by disease before the final battle began:

> 'It must be clear now – even to the Frenchman – that the Anglo-Saxon, and the Anglo-Saxon alone, is destined to carry civilisation to the Hindoo. Only the Saxon could carry

a calm front in the midst of savage hordes; give daily battle against fearful odds, and be the victor always; and, with a mere handful of armed men, subdue a revolted nation.'[32]

Havelock's manufactured legend was such that his biographer later described him in almost saintly terms:

> 'a Christian warrior of the right breed – a man of cool head and resolute heart, who has learned that the religion of war is to strike home and hard, with a single eye to God and his country'.[33]

Such was the public's affection for the general, based entirely though it was on sensationalist press reports, that they appealed for and then paid for his statue in Trafalgar Square. Even so, the media moved on and the public's predilection for distant war found other imperial adventures to follow, including Kitchener's in the Sudan three decades later.

Now Havelock is mostly forgotten; only the pigeons seem keen to bless his brow today, but militarist rhetoric still appeals to a polarised conception of conflict, in which each belligerent party casts itself as righteous and the other as barbaric. In light of *Lloyds Weekly*'s triumphalist report of civilisation's victory over savagery in India, consider what Paul Bremmer had to say, as head of the US Administration in Iraq in 2004, after the murder and subsequent defilement of four Americans:

> 'Yesterday's events in Fallujah are a dramatic example of the ongoing struggle between human dignity and barbarism… The acts we have seen were despicable and inexcusable. They violate the tenets of all religions including Islam, as well as the foundations of civilised society. Their deaths will not go unpunished.'[34]

A few hours later, the US would launch a massive retaliatory strike, *Operation Vigilant Resolve*, of which most fatalities were civilians including young children; thousands of people were displaced from their homes.[35]

Contemporary war is now relayed in, or close to, real-time. The realities of warfare do permeate the material we are shown, but the increasingly close collusion of media organisations with military authorities still fosters the notional sanitised, noble war. The 'war reporter' and 'investigative journalist' are becoming rare, which has made news organisations more dependent on official sources and the state's narrative. For example, although reporters seeking public opinion will often stand on a street corner and take a range of views from passers-by, they are not allowed to do this in a battalion of soldiers. Many troops do not believe the wars in Iraq and Afghanistan were just, but military authorities ensure that individuals selected for interview will toe the line with an anodyne statement, such as that they have a job to do and are looking forward to doing it. This becomes by default what we think soldiers think. I once asked a distinguished BBC war journalist what would happen if he interviewed a pair of British soldiers on the eve of a distant war and they told him they hated being there and just wanted to go home. Would the interview go to air that evening? No, he said.[36]

The academic Roger Stahl notes that as TV companies have become corporatised, they have ditched rigorous international news and investigation in favour of less costly content, such as opinion, entertainment, and health programmes.[37] Only 1% of US TV news time covered popular opposition during the build-up to the Gulf War in 1990, despite worldwide protest marches of hundreds of thousands of people.[38] Once the war began, journalists were concentrated in a single hotel and supplied with ready-to-air news. There they benefited from 'compelling footage, access to officials, updates, and human interest stories for free and at virtually no human risk', writes Roger Stahl.[39] There was precious little gathering of news in the traditional, investigative mode;[40] instead, journalists would package their distance from the war as proximity to it. Their reportage amounted to censorship by omission, further distancing the TV viewer from the realities of the warfare. In both senses of the term, the war was *screened* to the public.

In that war, news agencies were treated for the first time to that most consumable construct of war rhetoric: the 'surgical strikes' of 'precision warfare' in the 'clean war'. We were offered war without too much violence; war, in other words, for the squeamish. The cultural critic Slavoj Žižek situates this as a fad within the West's creeping culture of fussiness:

> 'On today's market, we find a series of products deprived of their malignant property: coffee without caffeine, cream without fat, beer without alcohol. The list goes on: virtual sex as sex without sex, the Colin Powell [former US Secretary of State] doctrine of war with no casualties (on our side, of course) as war without war, the redefinition of politics as expert administration as politics without politics.'[41]

The difference is that, unlike fat in milk, the violence of war properly deserves our revulsion, but mainstream media are wont to excise it from their output. As evidence of a clean war in the Gulf, the six -o'clock news showed footage of the latest hi-tech weaponry at work. From our living room armchairs we followed laser-guided munitions falling through the air, guided by white cross-hairs to a grainy, grey, anonymous polygon on the ground. The first-person perspective of the footage allowed us as spectators to imagine that we controlled the missile's flight, as in a videogame. As a teenager, I remember gazing vacantly at this on the TV news in a state of credulous stupor while semi-consciously willing the cross hairs to the left or the right so as to strike the target dead centre. There was a mild thrill to the experience, even while I was also wondering who was inside that angular shape at the time, and who their families were.

Captivating though this footage could be, it was a sham of the real war that we were being asked to support. Despite its repeated appearance on TV news, only 8% of all munitions used in the US air campaign were of a guided type.[42] One reason for this was financial. At the time of the war, a laser-guided bomb cost between $75,000 and $100,000,[43] a cruise missile more than $1 million.[44] A typical cluster bomb, such as the CBU-87, was cheap in comparison at around $14,000 and, unlike guided munitions, could destroy multiple targets in a wide area with its 202 free-fall bomblets.[45] Cluster bombs are everything that a precision strike is not meant to be – inaccurate, indiscriminate, and likely to leave unexploded ordnance strewn across the landscape, rendering it economically unproductive for years – but their use was extensive.[46] On TV we were treated to the reassuring spectacle of a clean war. The real, dirty war, in which undetonated bomblets would maim children months and years later, was hidden.

Just as during the Indian Rebellion of 1857, so in the Gulf War of 1990–91, the public were amazed by how modern communications seemed to bring them so close to witnessing war as it took place, while it actually continued to keep them distanced from the facts on the ground.

Militarism and modernity

In its fundamentals, much of this is not new; we have long indulged in an enjoyable fantasy of violence from a safe distance. Military and nationalistic parades, certain war toys and games, titillating press reports from distant conflicts, and imperially bleached histories and geographies have always contributed to an alienated conception of war in the public imagination.

Even so, modernity has new ways of distancing us from critical awareness of militarism and war. The changes that our age is undergoing also offer opportunities to build durable public resistance to war and its glorification, but some of these cut both ways; our now-relentless immersion in information is one. A century ago the government could use posters, newspapers, public meetings, the newsreel and the wireless to push out its message to the public. Now, communications media so saturate daily life that powerful social actors are able to integrate previously disparate instances of war propaganda into an integrated system of persuasion and manipulation. To this end, the ballooning military-industrial complex – the industrial war economy whose political sway Eisenhower warned us about half a century ago – now encompasses much of our cultural infrastructure. Large sections of the entertainment industry, children's education, academia, and the news media, are subject to varying degrees of control by interests invested in militarist worldviews and the wars that stem from them. The new militarist complex can now reach more people in more places at any time of day and at every stage of our lives with its fundamental message, which is that war is necessary, good, even enjoyable.

This trend flows with another: the growing influence of the economic system on culture, in which the tricks and tropes of a consumer-capitalist economy are used to package and promote notionally clean, necessary wars. By aiming to attach fantasy appeal to a consumer product and use it to eclipse whatever its practical merit may be, advertisers are selling fantasy rather than utility. The greatest achievement of their art is to commodify elusive human feelings and feed them back to us for a price. The McDonald's 'Happy Meal' cannot bring happiness for long, nor is it much of a meal; BMW do not manufacture joy, whatever their adverts may claim; and self-worth is not a cosmetic that you can buy just 'because you're worth it'. In similar fashion, war can be packaged as a spectacle: a pleasing but concocted image that attempts, cuckoo-like, to stand in for the real thing. The Help for Heroes logo now reaches consumers in the supermarket on a branded pack of 'Cheese for Heroes'. Bizarre though this is, it is easily understood as a natural extension of the commodification of desire, in this case a desire to mend war's harm and efface its violence. Perhaps it is only a matter of time before McDonald's brands Happy Meals with a military theme, so that you can consume, like extra relish on your burger, the reassurance that however violent war may be, our soldiers are going to be alright.

The philosopher Guy Debord explored the notion of a 'society of the spectacle' in his book of that name. Published in 1967, it described the cultural effects of 20th Century Western consumer economies and discussed two dynamics of social control embedded within them.[47] The first was 'ideological consumption', being the attractive packaging of ideas, like products for sale, that a credulous public then ingests and makes its own.[48] The other was 'concentrated and expanded alienation'; our growing collective immersion in the 'spectacle' at the expense of critical awareness of the world. Cheese for Heroes exemplifies both. It sells us a palatable conceit about the violence of war – that all will be well – while instrumentalising war for the manufacturer's profit. The tiny 7p charitable donation from each pack sold, though touted as the main purpose of the branding, is only a by-product.

Overall, Debord's critique of modern society was more pessimistic than it needed to be. We are indeed increasingly submerged in a hypnotic, consumer-capitalist reverie in which 'what appears is good; what is good appears',[49] but we are also human beings, not mere consumers, and not always as easily led by the nose as he implied. Even so, his case was strong: consumer-capitalism presents a captivating but unreal spectacle of pseudo-choices, through which existential questions of meaning, identity, and relationship, are mediated. Were Debord alive today, he would not be surprised to know that some 3,500 marketing messages go to work on the unconscious mind of the average urbanite each day, [50] nor that corporate retail giants have cloned themselves to occupy every town centre, dominating public space and occupying public consciousness. And he would not be surprised to see the same system used to create a spectacle of war.

Imagine war packaged as if it were a cultural commodity of its own, rather like a film or videogame. It could be called *Shock and Awe* with genuine military footage interposed with fictional scenes, all played by real-life troops. A lucrative merchandising deal could comprise a toy doll of the US President in combat gear, perhaps, to symbolise the warrior nation, and the public could join in with 'Support Our Troops' bumper-stickers and 'Future soldier' t-shirts for children. Perhaps some of these ideas seem far-fetched, but they have all been realised already.

Noble war, clean war, enjoyable war, spectacular war. Within the diminished horizons of these various fabrications, there is no room for the idea that war might be 'organised murder', as First World War veteran Harry Patch put it, and 'not worth one [lost life] let alone the millions'.[51] If Western societies' anodyne, consumer-friendly spectacle of war continues unchecked, it is bound to distance us further from recognising, as disciplined witnesses would, that the central activity of warfare is mass violence – bodies tearing at bodies. A critical appreciation of war, grounded as it has to be in its disturbing realities, is the least we owe to the Margret Freyers caught up in today's and tomorrow's conflicts.

Limits of the lie

As humane human beings, and as societies with a tradition of peace as well as war, we are apt to revolt against extreme violence when we recognise it for what it is. Even when war is geographically distant, testimonies, histories and journalism that centre on stories of ordinary people affected, rather than only on the abstracted machinations of politicians and generals, can focus our understanding on war where it actually happens. Whereas an alienated people is easily co-opted as war's armchair sponsors, our alienation fluctuates, persisting by degrees, not absolutely. The state and its allies have to throw millions of pounds of our money into spinning a consumable version of war and making its militarised foreign policy publicly acceptable. Their success is remarkably patchy; they know it and they worry about it.

Even children – perhaps especially children – are capable of resisting glib representations of militarism and warfare. In 2013, London's Museum of Childhood curated an exhibition of 'War Games', showing a wide range of mostly war-glorifying toys from the last 100 years or so. The curators welcomed children with the claim that 'real warfare and changing weapons technology are accurately mirrored in toys and games'.[52] In so doing, they muddled a realistic idea of war with a merely convincing one, but children who visited the exhibition were not as confused. At the end of the exhibition, having poked and prodded the few items that they were allowed to touch, children were invited to fill out cards printed with 'I think war games are…' and pin them up. Besides some flippant contributions, several of their notes showed their wariness about the casual use of war to inspire games and toys. Jack, aged 6½, wrote:

'I think war games are… bad because we're just making a joke when it really happened!' An anonymous card read: 'I think war games are… dangerous because it can get you into war.' Another reflected a child's sensitivity to the pathos of war: 'I think war games are… sad. People should talk not fight. War games makes killing a game. That is sad.' Whilst young children play at war, they can also be sensitively critical of the real thing.

Among older children and their parents' generation, the government's strenuous efforts to convert widespread veneration of the British soldier into new enlistments and popular support for Britain's wars have largely come to nothing. Armed forces recruitment has been in steady decline, with annual intake of the youngest – those aged 16 and 17 – showing the most marked fall from around 8,215 a decade ago to 2,120 now.[53]

It is clear now that the US-led, UK-supported invasions in Afghanistan and Iraq have been disastrous for the people of both countries, as well as for families of Coalition troops killed or severely injured. In Britain, as elsewhere, both actions went ahead despite opposition from the majority of the public, much of it manifest in widespread, active protest. The government was aided significantly by a mostly supine response from parliament and a gung-ho press. Seen in this light, one story of these wars has to be a pessimistic one for a country that likes to think of itself as democratic and progressive. But another story is also possible: of a government and military anxious that the public are increasingly sceptical about British wars abroad. In response, the government has hastily grasped at a host of policy initiatives to ensure that the public 'understands and appreciates' what the armed forces do.[54] This is a mark not so much of an overweening state but one fearful that its public are not where it needs them to be.

Why has the consumable, spectacular version of war, which is so culturally ubiquitous, failed to coax the public into supporting policy on Iraq and Afghanistan? One answer is that the state now finds it much harder to keep the public distanced from the realities of war. After massive worldwide protests in anticipation of the Iraq War, negative news stories of the war's course have been relentless, even in media outlets supportive of government policy. When al-Jazeera callously aired footage of British soldiers killed early in the Iraq War, the public were shocked and disgusted, as was Tony Blair,[55] although British TV news had not balked at showing corpses of enemy forces. There were justifiable complaints that the Qatari news station had broken the Geneva Conventions, which regulate the treatment of Prisoners of War and the corpses of combatants, but this was after Coalition Forces determined that captured insurgents would not be accorded Prisoner of War status at all. These double-standards and more-than-usually graphic presentations of war's brutality became broadcast news beyond the government's control.

Indeed, reports of civilian deaths, maimings and bereavements appeared almost daily. Wounded, wailing children hit the headlines, including five-year-old Samar Hassan, whose parents were killed by American troops at a checkpoint in Iraq. She was shockingly pictured crying out and with her hands bleeding while surrounded by US soldiers in a pool of light in a concrete room.[56] Faced with many similar images, as well as widespread unrest in Iraq broadcast across the world, US Defense Secretary Donald Rumsfeld scoffed, 'Henny Penny – "The sky is falling."'[57] But his famous cocksure sarcasm dissolved into exasperation with the media for not sticking to his story of 'a country that's being liberated'.[58] Against his hopes, pictures of injured innocents pricked the public conscience, raising sharp questions about the cavalier military tactics and lax rules of engagement that he was responsible for.

As the wars in Iraq and Afghanistan went on, it became clear that they had slipped the restraints of International Humanitarian Law, as wars always do. The torture and ritual humiliation of Iraqi detainees at Abu Ghraib, the draconian incarceration and vindictive treatment of prisoners without charge in Guantánamo Bay, the exponential increase in shady covert US special forces operations, and leaked stories of anonymous Iraqis rendered (kidnapped) to 'black sites' for torture, all served to expose the dirty war agenda. When whistle-blower Chelsea (formerly Bradley) Manning leaked the hidden details of US forces' belligerence, she opened a can of worms all over her government and was punished with a 35-year sentence. Among her leaked material was a military film showing the murder by US Apache helicopters of an Iraqi film crew and then of the passers-by who stopped to tend to them.[59] Suspicions emerged of British complicity in rendition, and although British troops mostly operated within the law on the battlefield, some did not. After a group of British soldiers tortured a group of apparently innocent Iraqis – including Baha Mousa, whom they beat to death – the accused then scuppered their trial by closing ranks against the judge and clamming up.[60] The government managed to pass the incident off as the work of a few bad apples, but not before the appalling episode had added to public scepticism about the war.

News bulletins announced British forces fatalities from morning to night. During the most intense fighting of the Afghanistan War, reports were airing daily of soldiers – some aged just 18 – being killed by roadside bombs or small arms fire. Many British soldiers were coming home injured; by 2014 there had been in the region of 2,500 battle-wounded casualties in Iraq and Afghanistan.[61] More still were experiencing problems with mental health and violent behaviour, particularly young men in front-line roles.[62]

Some veterans were leaving the forces, writing exposés, speaking out on prime-time television, and turning to anti-militarist activism. Ben Griffin, who participated in SAS 'night raids' on Iraqi homes and was stopped by the courts from talking about it, established Veterans for Peace UK. The organisation and its growing membership has since strongly resisted British involvement in the wars and challenged the militarisation of society. Joe Glenton, author of the award-winning memoir *Soldier Box*, has written a number of politically incisive, unsettling commentaries on aspects of Britain's military institutions and its wars. While some journalists were cheerfully regurgitating the official PR for Prince Harry's stage-managed tour of Afghanistan, others were hungry for these sources of emerging dissent among veterans.

Despite the moral confusion and human wreckage of the wars, armed forces recruitment materials still promised a noble career of humanitarian purpose. They described a military lifestyle as much like a civilian one, albeit with marching, white-water rafting, and patriotic, life-saving missions thrown in. To mums and dads deciding whether to let their children enlist, the virtually risk-free picture of the humanitarian soldier tidily delivering 'decisive strikes' against 'enemy weak spots'[63] in the national interest must have seemed increasingly at odds with reality.

Meanwhile, doubts about the long-term strategy were widely voiced. The failure of the British mission in Basra and the bogged-down counter-insurgency in Helmand prompted a stream of reports about poor equipment, but calls for better flak jackets and armoured personnel carriers missed the underlying flaw. The problem was that both campaigns were unwinnable – 'beyond our powers,' as the military historian Max Hastings bluntly said of Afghanistan in 2009.[64] Stratospheric financial costs also spoiled the state's narrative. A Harvard University study in 2013 estimated that both wars would eventually cost the American taxpayer at least $4 trillion once long-term care of injured veterans was included – a staggering sum for a country mired in extreme economic inequality.[65] A similar estimate for the financial liability to the UK has not been carried out, but official estimates have put the cost of the wars in Iraq and Afghanistan at £8.2 billion (to early 2010) and £25 billion (to mid-2013) respectively.[66] As these figures exclude regular Defence budget items such as wages, as well as all costs not yet incurred, they are substantial under-estimates.

Faced with these apparent contradictions, only a diminishing few still held the line that a straightforwardly just, clean war – that is, the *spectacular war* – was taking place. Whether or not the campaigns in Iraq and Afghanistan were argued to be necessary, no one could deny that they were a military and moral quagmire. The diverse efforts of investigative journalists, anti-war direct activists, disaffected veterans and their families, politically engaged artists, small citizen actions and, most importantly, voices of Iraqi and Afghan civilians, had successfully disrupted the official narrative. In effect, the persistent action of the wars' detractors helped to bridge the imaginative distance between the public and the violence they were being asked to support. Yes, this undermined troops' morale, but only because political leaders had sent them to war on the back of a spectacle of shaky lies and had expected the public to remain largely unaware of the brutality of warfare. By contrast, it took years for stories like Margret Freyer's to reach the pages of English history books after the Second World War.

Scepticism about the campaigns in Afghanistan and Iraq paralleled an altogether contrary trend: growing support for the armed forces. In 2008, a Mori poll found that 81% of the public viewed the forces favourably;[67] if the wars were a mess, our boys and girls were not to blame. That the public would 'support our troops' but not what they were doing worried the architects of the wars. In 2007, Tony Blair protested that 'the armed forces want public opinion not just behind them but behind their mission'; we should 'understand their value not just their courage', he declaimed.[68] Military bosses were concerned, too. In 2009, the Chief of Defence Staff, Jock Stirrup, claimed rather implausibly that the Taliban's roadside bombs were less of a threat to troops' morale than 'declining will' among the public to see the war won.[69] 'Support for our servicemen and women is indivisible from support for this mission,' he said,[70] although had that been true, it would not have needed saying.

State militarism, public scepticism: story of a provincial town

Perhaps proponents and detractors of the wars have both been wrong to expect that a casual, flag-waving militarism goes hand-in-glove with high rates of enlistment or resolute public support for specific wars. Public attitudes to Britain's wars are layered and complex. Parents of potential recruits, for example, will not necessarily allow them to enlist at 16 just because the family waves Union flags at the Red Arrows on Armed Forces Day. The complexity – and sometimes confusion – of public attitudes has been shown nowhere more clearly than at Wootton Bassett in Wiltshire, where the initially spontaneous repatriation ceremonies became a political cauldron that the government and establishment press could not control.

The ceremonies began in 2007 when Percy Miles, a former town mayor and veteran, stood alone in his mayoral robes while a military hearse drove down the High Street. His gesture far from glorified the Afghanistan war; he was opposed to it outright.[71] Other locals then also felt moved to bear witness to the hearses – sometimes a long line of them – passing through the town. Margaret Friend, a shopkeeper, told the BBC:

> 'The side of it we see here in Bassett: they [the troops] shouldn't be out there. That's what we think anyway. Talk to anyone in the town and I'm pretty sure they'd all say the same... a lot of these guys [the dead] are only 18, 20...'[72]

The mayor, Steve Bucknell, said later that these acts of remembrance were 'totally divorced from politics'.[73] If they were, they did not stay that way. Thousands of visitors soon flocked to the town to line the 46-mile route on 'repat days'. Journalists swarmed in with 'helicopters and vans and cherry pickers', according to Margaret Friend, pointing cameras into the faces of mourning families.[74] They 'took away the dignity of the tribute', said the council leader, Chris Wannell.[75] *The Sun* called the town the most patriotic in Britain;[76] a petition to rename the procession route Highway for Heroes gathered signatures; and the British National Party leader Nick Griffin turned up. Islam4UK announced, then withdrew, their intention to march through the town in protest at the war. Steve Bucknell reflected: 'For some reason the rest of the world found this [act of remembrance] fascinating and I began to question myself whether we were doing the right thing after all.'[77] Despite their doubts, the townspeople determined to persist with their quiet tribute amid the political bluster and mawkish tourists.

Stuart Griffiths, a photographer and artist who recorded the repatriation days and is a veteran himself, summarised what had become a national phenomenon:

> 'Wootton Bassett has become unfortunately a "double sided sword" which I interpret as a media spectacle and

circus and a focal point for people who are dictated by a media (such as the *Daily Mail* and *Sun*) on how we should live our lives – but also there is a sense of honour and confusion (to the current British troop involvement overseas) which is very much a reflection of the real state of the UK at present.'[78]

The town's representatives told the media that residents did not want 'pomp' or 'militarisation' and they rejected talk of conferring royal status on the town.[79] The government gave it to them anyway, as well as a name-changing ceremony complete with a visiting royal, plastic flags for children to wave, and RAF fly-by. The state, hitherto side-lined, clearly hoped to encompass the town's actions in its own narrative about the good war. David Cameron said that the town's 'respect and mourning have shown the deep bond between the public and our armed forces'.[80] This was a fair statement, except for omitting that the town was also becoming an emblem of public disquiet about the war. Indeed, the armed forces and the government were worried that the town's witness to the dead was exposing the war's harm to families and communities at home. General Richard Dannatt, the head of the army at the time, said later:

> 'The Wootton Bassett factor runs the risk of undermining morale of the population at home and fuelling the bring the boys home agenda, which potentially means that we would lose the hearts and minds battle here at home.'[81]

For the government's part, a leaked MoD report warned that repatriation ceremonies were making the public 'risk-averse' and recommended reducing their public profile.[82] The public must be 'won over to accepting the implications of using the Armed Forces', it said. Not for the first time, public scepticism about the war was cast in terms of moral weakness, rather than compassion or common sense. Even so, the government was right to worry;

the US government was having fewer such problems, having prudently banned the media presence at repatriation sites, first in 1990 for the Gulf War and then again for the Iraq War.[83]

Power of the pinprick

The organisational threads of war-making in late-capitalist societies are frail; they depend not only on the continuous active participation of combatants but also on the sustained support of the public, or at least our passive acquiescence. The nation rides to war on a vainglorious spectacle, but like the ball of hot air it is, the lie can be punctured by a pinprick. By the asymmetric nonviolence of simple actions, euphemisms are de-robed, contradictions lampooned, the true costs of war laid out for none to ignore. The lie is turned against itself, however much gold the state throws into the show. The voices of people that war most affects – civilians and veterans – are brought to the surface of public awareness and so the humanity at the heart of war, and its inhumanity, are named and reclaimed. Articulate counter-narratives embarrass the sterile official PR, denude the militarist rhetoric of the political élite, and expose the cheapo jingo of the mainstream press as shrill and thoughtless. If this cannot turn the national story of the glorious war into one about the actual war, then it is at least to heckle again and again during the telling, mangling the cultural machinery of the lie.

Veterans know that lie more than most. 25 years after the Falklands War, Gus Hales joined a week-long veterans' pilgrimage to the islands. The trip concluded on Remembrance Sunday with a service in Port Stanley's cathedral, where the front three pews had been reserved for civic dignitaries, military brass and a government minister, Derek Twigg. To Gus's mind, the establishment's story about the war was distanced from the experiences of the ordinary soldiers who had gone through the thick of the violence, and whose voices were seldom heard. As silence fell after prayers of intercession, he stood, walked to the front and recited his poem before anyone could stop him:

Deep In My Mind Where Nobody Goes

Every year on Remembrance Sunday
I sit in the corner of a British Legion Bar
Dressed in blazer, shirt, Regimental tie
Polished shoes, with my head held high.

But deep in my mind, where nobody goes
I see a wooden cross where the wind of victory blows.
'Three Cheers for Victory,' I heard the politician say.
But they never asked me about my victory.
And if they did, I would have explained it this way:

It isn't your flags or the emblems of war
Or the marching of troops past the Palace's door.
It isn't Mrs Thatcher on the balcony high
Reaffirming her pledge to serve or die.

But it's the look and the pain on a teenager's face
As he dies for his country, in a far off place.
It's the guns and the shells and the Phosphorus grenades,
The dead and the wounded, the freshly cut graves

Or the grieving wife with a fatherless child,
Whose young, tender life will be forever defiled
Or the alcoholic soldier with a shattered mind
Who takes the suicide option for some peace to find.
Well that's my victory, but no one knows
For it's deep in my mind where nobody goes.[84]

When he finished, everyone was on their feet applauding, except
for those sat in the front three rows, and the vicar, who looked on
in silence.

Dresden

Brought up on film clips of the London Blitz, we might imagine that more British than German civilians suffered in the bombing campaigns of the Second World War. In fact, the opposite is true: 60,000 people in Britain were killed by German raids; Allied (mostly RAF) bombers killed around 800,000 people in Germany.[85] The difference is due partly to Britain's huge industrial investment in bombing, but also the Air Ministry's policy of aiming to destroy civilian population centres. The Luftwaffe would also target civilians, but in general went after military and other strategically significant targets, typically further away from city centres.

On both sides, almost all casualties of the city-centre bombings were women, children and the elderly; the attacks were atrocities. The road to the most notorious of these – the Dresden Massacre of 1945 – begins elsewhere, in Iraq during the interwar years. The country was then a British protectorate managed by a puppet dictator who faced a number of popular rebellions against his authoritarian rule. In 1920, one such uprising was crushed by British forces using a tactic it would later condemn Saddam Hussein for repeating: directly targeting population centres with air power.[86] Winston Churchill, then responsible for Iraq as Minister of the Colonies, had pushed for the use of air raids against civilians so that he could draw down his troops garrisoned there and control the country more cheaply.[87] Eventually, Britain pacified the rebellious Iraqis, which allowed British Petroleum to lead a consortium of oil companies with exclusive extraction rights in the country – an arrangement that lasted until Saddam nationalised Iraqi oil production in 1972.[88]

British air raids in Iraq enabled Hugh Trenchard, then responsible for air power in the country, to test his theory that bombing residential areas would cause the enemy to capitulate more quickly than destroying military targets.[89] Later called the Trenchard Doctrine, this theory would provide the strategy, such as it was, for the air war against Germany. It also inspired another British officer stationed in 1920s Iraq, Arthur Harris, who would lead RAF Bomber Command two decades later.[90]

From 1942, Arthur Harris ordered raids by more than a thousand bombers at a time against German cities. By the time of the Dresden attack, the city centres of Cologne, Hamburg and several others had already been levelled. Just one month of raids against Hamburg in 1943 killed a similar number of civilians as died across the whole of Britain during the entire war.[91] By codenaming that attack *Operation Gomorrah*, after the biblical city condemned by God for its sin, British commanders rhetorically framed the massacre in terms of righteous retribution. The strategic rationale for these raids, wrote Harris, was

> 'the destruction of German cities, the killing of German workers and the disruption of civilised community life throughout Germany. It should be emphasised that the destruction of houses, public utilities, transport and lives, the creation of a refugee problem on an unprecedented scale, and the breakdown of morale both at home and at the battle fronts by fear of extended and intensified bombing, are accepted and intended aims of our bombing policy. They are not by-products of attempts to hit factories.'[92]

For these attacks against residential centres, Allied planes were loaded with a mix of high-explosive and incendiary bombs. The aim was to create an uncontrollable firestorm, in which the city would burn up as a whole.[93] Rapidly-rising, superheated air would suck the surrounding atmosphere towards the fires, causing tornado-force winds and ambient temperatures – even at some distance from the flames – sufficient to incinerate people as they fled through the streets or cowered in cellars. In places, the winds were strong enough to lift and hurl a person into the flames. Those not burnt alive would asphyxiate as the fire consumed all the available oxygen.

Humanitarian concerns in Britain about the bombing policy were dismissed: 'I do not personally regard the whole of the remaining cities of Germany worth the bones of one British Grenadier,' wrote Arthur Harris.[94] Yet his and others' insistence on the necessity of the policy flew in the face of its manifest strategic failure. The mass bombing of civilians had devastated German families and communities but had little effect on the Nazi war machine. By the time of the Dresden attack in February 1945, three years of the Trenchard Doctrine had failed to cause the enemy to capitulate. Nonetheless, Churchill, the Air Ministry and Bomber Command persisted in ordering raids on the residential hearts of German cities while often leaving military targets intact on the outskirts.

As a million or so frostbitten and starving German refugees fled before the Russian advance in late 1944, Harris advocated bombing their likely places of safety in order to maximise civil chaos.[95] Dresden was on the list. The city had little military-strategic significance, except for its railway and Autobahn; as neither was targeted, both survived. The attack appears to have had a politically strategic motive, however. With the war's end in sight, the three major Allied powers were to meet in Yalta in early 1945 to negotiate control of the post-war world, especially Europe. Stalin and Roosevelt were the main parties to this; Churchill, at the head of a waning empire, was losing his leverage.[96] Churchill had asked the Air Ministry for plans for 'basting the Germans in their retreat' from the Russian front.[97] Harris's proposed Dresden raid was approved, timed to coincide with the Yalta meeting. In the event, bad weather delayed the attack until after the talks had ended, so if the raid had a political purpose, it was lost.

The raid was based on three waves of attack targeted at the residential city centre. The first wave of RAF Lancaster bombers would start the fires and overwhelm local capacity to douse them; the second wave would create a self-sustaining firestorm; the third, this time by the US Air Force, would continue bombing while long-range fighter planes strafed targets of opportunity. All went according to plan. Alexander McKee collected testimonies from survivors for his book about the raid and its aftermath. While the RAF bomber crews were heading home from Dresden, Annemarie Waehmann, aged 20, was trying to escape the fires:

'[It] was indescribable, horrible … It looked like a crater landscape, and then we saw the dead. Charred or carbonised bodies, shrunk to half size. Oh, dear God! At the Freiburger Platz we saw an ambulance, with a number of male nurses about to put a stretcher into it. A number of people were sitting on the ground. But why didn't they move? As we came nearer, we saw it all. They were all dead. Their lungs had been burst by the blast.'

Margret Freyer, having narrowly survived the flames, though badly burnt, went through the streets looking for her fiancé.

'I looked for him amongst the dead, because hardly any living beings were to be seen anywhere. What I saw is so horrific that I shall hardly be able to describe it. Dead, dead, dead everywhere. Some completely black like charcoal. Others completely untouched, lying as if they were asleep. Women in aprons, women with children sitting in the trams as if they had just nodded off [these had probably died from asphyxiation]. Many women, many young girls, many small children, soldiers who were only identifiable as such by the metal buckles on their belts, almost all of them naked. Some clinging to each other in groups as if they were clawing at each other.'[98]

The same morning, the US Air Force arrived for the third attack wave. By this point, the bombers were mostly just rearranging rubble, but fighter planes swept down repeatedly to machine-gun the burnt and injured refugees as they fled from the city across the fields in their hundreds.[99]

The deliberate area-bombing of civilians in Germany, France, Britain and elsewhere during the Second World War would meet most modern definitions of terrorism today, albeit on a scale far greater than any non-state terrorist attack has ever achieved. Whilst some of the bomber crews had misgivings about the policy, the men who ordered the attacks for Britain were unrepentant. Arthur Harris said that the qualms some people had after the Dresden raid 'could be easily explained by any psychiatrist'.[100]

Some of the post-war examination of the Dresden bombing has characterised it as a one-off atrocity perpetrated by Arthur Harris, but this is wrong. Dresden was not an aberration, but only the worst of many abominable air raids against civilians based on the official policy of the time. Bomber Command had begun the war with a more restrained targeting policy, but the passage of time showed the tendency of warfare to escalate and to amplify its violence, breaking free from whatever humanitarian limits may have been imposed at its outset. Further testament to this was still to come in the nuclear attacks against the people of Hiroshima and Nagasaki later the same year. The massacre of civilians was the avowed policy of other war leaders, too, with Hitler the worst among them. The officially sanctioned targeting of civilian population centres has continued as a feature of many other wars around the world since 1945, including those in the former Yugoslavia, Afghanistan and Iraq.

Arthur Harris was not solely, or even mainly, responsible for the Dresden bombing. He proposed it, devised it, and justified it afterwards to the world, but his superiors in the hierarchy had all enthusiastically agreed the policy of attacking civilian centres. Charles Portal as head of the RAF, Archibald Sinclair as Secretary of State for Air, and Winston Churchill as Prime Minister, supported the policy unwaveringly throughout the war. Hugh Trenchard had argued for it from his seat in the Lords. It also had the blessing and encouragement of Churchill's Scientific Adviser, Frederick Lindemann. He wanted bombers to concentrate their attacks in working class areas, where population density was greatest; the hope was that half of all houses in the major cities would be razed.[101] Most of Parliament and the Church, including the Archbishop of Canterbury, supported it. The only two prominent public figures in outspoken opposition at the time – Richard Stokes MP and the Bishop of Chichester, George Bell – were more or less shouted down by their peers and pilloried in the press.[102] So, Arthur Harris was not alone; the British

Ypres, Belgium, after the Battle of Passchendaele, 1917 (Photo: Frank Hurley)

*Cologne, Germany, after the Operation Millennium 1,000-bomber raid, 1942
(Photo: US Army)*

Dresden, Germany, after the 1,000-bomber raid originally code-named Operation Thunderclap, 1945 (Photo: Sächsische Landesbibliothek, Dresden)

Fallujah, Iraq, after Operation Phantom Fury destroyed a quarter of the city's 39,000 homes, 2004 (Photo: US Marine Corps)

establishment in general supported the sustained, mass-killing of German civilians.

What principle of human nature or culture leads educated people to support a barbaric and strategically ineffective policy with such unflinching resolve? Perhaps Britain's war leaders, who were drawn from a rarefied, all-male, social élite with an imperial worldview, were empathically too distant from the fate of working class people in another country, who were deemed expendable collateral in the cause of defeating the Third Reich. Or perhaps the insidious logic of war, as it shifts the culture of what is considered normal and thus acceptable, confuses our moral sense in ways that are problematic to judge from a peace-time perspective.

Whatever the culpabilities may be of the leadership that ordered the bombing of German civilians, should we applaud as war heroes the men who order atrocities? Churchill, Portal and Sinclair were, like Harris, all knighted; London now boasts statues to all but Sinclair. When the Harris statue was unveiled in 1992, *The Daily Mail* dubbed its critics 'peace idiots'.[103] If a long war had alienated these men from what they were doing, how much more alienated are we to celebrate them now that the facts are in and we know what they did?

ROMANCE

To a political realist, war is merely a means to an end; it becomes more or less justified insofar as it is more or less effective in achieving its purpose. In like manner, governments support their decisions to fight war by appealing to reason. War is presented as a way to keep us safe, protect our interests abroad, maintain access to natural resources, liberate the oppressed. More privately, governments also admit the utility of war to maintain strategic alliances, redraw the political map, or open new markets for corporations. Those of us who believe war is so horrific that it must be judged as an end in itself, and not just as a means to one, propose counter-arguments in similarly rational terms. War kills more people than it saves; it rarely results in anything other than more violence; its true purposes are more self-serving than the defensive or humanitarian patina that governments coat it with.

Whilst such rationalist discourse matters, it overlooks that wars are also the fruit of passion. Our own culture romances war, fantasising about it in gushing hyperbole that is anything but rational or reasonable. It is not dispassionate reason that leads mainstream media to call soldiers 'heroes' for no other reason than that they are soldiers, George W Bush to characterise the war in Afghanistan as a 'crusade',[104] or Tony Blair to 'feel a most urgent sense of mission about today's world' after the invasion of Iraq.[105] The calm deliberations of reason are a world away when governments extol their own self-righteousness – as 'a beacon of hope',[106] for example – and damn their opponents as untouchable, as an 'axis of evil arming to threaten the peace of the world'.[107] Nor is it rational to presume that any prospective action other than violence would be weak, such as when George W Bush claimed in 2002 that 'some governments will be timid in the face of terror'.[108] Tony Blair presented the same false war-or-weakness dichotomy a year later:

'But if we show weakness now, if we allow the plea for more time to become just an excuse for prevarication until the moment for action passes, then it will not only be Saddam who is repeating history. The menace, and not just from Saddam, will grow; the authority of the UN will be lost; and the conflict when it comes will be more bloody.'[109]

Language like this shows how the psyche, and thus our culture, are wont to stylise war as an heroic quest. The terms used – crusade, mission, hero, urgent, menace – recast war as an idealised, romantic story that valorises violence as righteous and even appealing. We inherit this story from thousands of years of culture.

The heroic quest

A millennium ago, a 'romance' was any story of heroic chivalry told around the fire. From *Sir Gawain and the Green Knight*, through *Sleeping Beauty* to modern-day James Bond films, the form is one everyone recognises, described here by the cultural critic Northrop Frye:

'The complete form of the romance is clearly the successful quest, and such a completed form has three main stages: the stage of the perilous journey and the preliminary minor adventures; the crucial struggle, usually some kind of battle in which either the hero or his foe, or both, must die; and the exaltation of the hero.'[110]

Frye roots the romance-quest historically in the ancient, ritualised, to-and-fro struggle between the fertile order of summer and the ever-threatening wasteland of winter.[111] As he describes the ritual, each shift of the seasons brings a hero from the upper world and a dark figure from the lower world to play out their conflict here, among us. By enacting this ritually, following the earth's own rhythms, our ancestors would imagine themselves sustaining and embodying the dynamic equilibrium of the cosmos.

Although Frye ties today's romance-quest to seasonal rituals, forms of heroic, cosmic struggles for order are common to many cultures. More than three millennia ago, the people of the Indus Valley ritually re-enacted creation stories in which gods imposed order on nebulous matter; the thunder god Indra slays the cloud demon Vitra by his lightning dart, for example.[112] The heroic conquest turns up again in the cultures of the ancient Near-East; the Babylonians sang of the watery chaos of Tiamat, whose reign was ended by the trepidatious Marduk in a mighty battle, bringing order from which the world of form could emerge.[113] Order is also imposed on formlessness in *Genesis*, making it a foundational narrative for Judaism, Christianity and Islam. The same mythic idea appears later in the Christianised story of St George and the Dragon, in which a warrior-crusader slays the wild beast of paganism and, psychically, the masculine dominates the feminine. Similar heroic battles were a major form in oral traditions that told the stories of *Beowulf* and *The Epic of Gilgamesh*.

Despite the ubiquity of this mythic conquest throughout these cultural traditions, all also ritualised stories that celebrated society's nurturers, preserved the mutuality of social (and also ecological) relationships, and reminded the tribe of its humility before the mysteries of nature, which were deemed godly. These countervailing narratives, in prizing communion and conciliation over conquest, would have tempered the tribe's preoccupation with control and order, which was necessary but also needed limiting.

Since those ancient ritual traditions, the cultural salience of conquest and domination stories has continued to wax and wane with the prevailing mood of the times. From the late 19th century, stories of similar outline have been the staple of adventure books and comics in Europe and America, for example. Their cultural influence deepened again with the advent of that most potently mesmeric of modern media: the Hollywood film. The action-adventure, which is the most popular film genre among teenagers,[114] is built on the same mythic quest-conquest, in which a hero deploys violence to correct some kind of evildoing and restore order.

We romanticise violence and war in many ways. Martial themes inspire fashion and music, the design of children's playgrounds,[115] and even food products, such as the British Legion-branded Forces Sauces 'serve with pride' tomato ketchup.[116] All these shape in small ways our conception of war, but Hollywood's power is unique as the pre-eminent storyteller of the world's dominant cultural and political tradition: Western consumer-capitalist society led by the United States. From this lofty mount, film-makers shape stories for us to tell about ourselves and 'the other', about the precarious order of the world, and about the role of violence in rupturing it and restoring it again. They rework time-worn stories and fashion new ones while shaped by all manner of influences, not least the corporate interests of their employers and the prevailing political order of the day. Thus, for young people in particular, Hollywood fills out our cultural imaginarium – the vast psychic store-house of stories that we use to make sense of our experience of the world.

Hollywood's romance-quest narrative operates psychologically, culturally and politically to shape and justify militarist values and worldviews. The man-hero who saves the day legitimates hyper-masculine behaviours and narrow gender identities, and prepares the young of the Western world for recruitment into their armed forces. The redemptive value attached to violence reinforces facile assumptions that our security depends on military force, rather than on structural justice and an ecology of mutual relationships. By aligning the moral order of the world with, usually, a version of US state power, Hollywood reinforces the notion that America's imperium is the generous and necessary guarantor of our freedoms. Hollywood's filmic devices are so culturally influential that they are even assumed into the rhetorical performance of politics. Life truly imitates art as British and US politicians frame real wars in terms barely distinguishable from those used in action-adventure films.

Some of these influences are explored here, before a brief look at three recent mainstream films that partially subvert the dominant heroic-quest narrative. These films show that points of cultural resistance to militarism also exist, even in Hollywood.

The man-hero-saviour

The Hollywood action film is really a drama about order. It begins typically with some kind of disturbance that holds our society at risk. Enter the hero, who appears as an incarnation of the knightly prince to redeem the drama by saving the situation and allaying our fear. Perhaps he is indeed a knight, as in *Kingdom of Heaven*, or has another formal martial or semi-martial role, as do James Bond the spy, Captain America the soldier, and John McClane, *Die Hard*'s off-duty cop. Perhaps he is no such thing, but thrust into gallantry by circumstance, as a father out to rescue his abducted family, for example, in *Unknown*. In any case, he is almost always a man.

The hero meets the disturbance personified as the villain, usually another man. The encounter tests the hero, who prevails by canniness, moral endurance and, usually, adept violence. The chaos that threatened the world is pushed back through the breach whence it came and the rupture in the fragile skin of order is made good – for now. The hero's reward is the right to be a man: as a lover of otherwise unattainable women, as a future king, or simply as a hero-saviour whom the masses honour with gratitude.

For the psyche, particularly that of an adolescent boy, the romance-quest is a story of wish-fulfilment. It allows him to imagine himself the hero – personally powerful and socially successful. The cultural historian Graham Dawson argues that the romance-quest answers a specific need of adolescent spectators to manage the tensions in their gender identity. Drawing on the work of the psychoanalyst Melanie Klein, he suggests that a young person is trying to balance two needs. The first is to fit in with external social demands based on pre-determined notions of masculine and feminine. The second is to act on internal feelings and impulses which simplistic notions of gender cannot contain.[117] The tension of these two needs is seen when a young boy who wants to play nurse is told he should play doctor 'because you're the boy'. He is faced with having either to insist on his wish for the sake of his authenticity, or to relinquish it and be accepted by others. Thus, the boy experiences his gender identity as a dilemma between needing to be who he is and needing to belong.

Girls face similar gendered dilemmas, although the teenage boy is additionally particularly preoccupied with his personal power and its limits. He feels he must not only be himself, but also prove himself. His life thus far has shaped him, but now he is anxious to shape it in turn: to be attractive and popular, to assert his interests effectively, and to imagine his future and its success. In this cause, he is drawn to whatever suitable stories from his culture that he can imagine as his own and use to order his world.

Into the breach strides the dominant male role-model figure in popular teen culture: the questing hero. On the big screen, films like *Superman, Batman, Spiderman, Iron Man, Mission Impossible,* and the James Bond and Jason Bourne franchises, jostle with thousands of others to present the heroic role as a paragon of traditional masculine virtues – stoicism, honour, physical strength. If an ordinary man is not man enough, he is enhanced by science, as is *Captain America,* or by accident of supernature, as in *Superman.* Whatever superficially character-enhancing weaknesses his creators may have bestowed on him – enfeebling kryptonite or a bit of a drink problem – he still appears true to himself, admired by all, and self-reliantly powerful, all at once. Blessed with apparent authenticity, social acceptability, and potency to shape the world, he easily presents an appealing role model for adolescent boys: the man-hero who does well in the world, whom everyone loves, and who gets to blow stuff up.

Whilst there are many superficially non-standard variants – when the hero prevails with little violence, or his mission requires a woman's help, or his vulnerability plays a role in the redemptive narrative – these typically amount to little more than minor diversions from the main theme. In this way, the romance-quest presents order, freedom and security as the achievement of traditional masculine roles, thus promoting one kind of role as supreme and marginalising others. The romance-quest teaches that we owe our security to the hyper-masculine man and his conquests, rather than to cooperation and conciliation, and to the nurturers of a just and generous society.

Whereas the ancient ritual of the passing seasons described by Northrop Frye prominently involved women, the community as a whole, and forms of power held to be feminine, Hollywood loses these in translation. The burden of salvation falls typically, sometimes ludicrously, to a lone warrior-man. In the high-grossing flag-waver *Olympus has Fallen*, an ex-Secret Service agent single-handedly retakes a bashed-up White House from a squad of North Korean élite paramilitaries, killing them all himself while still finding time to smuggle the President's child to safety. Another man, the rescued President, then completes the film with a speech to the nation in which he announces the restoration of American order:

> 'Our foe did not come only to destroy our things or our people, they came to desecrate a way of life, to foul our beliefs, trample our freedom ... They granted us the greatest gift – a chance at our rebirth. We will rise renewed...'

In that film, as in countless others, women play little or no role in redeeming the fallen world. The young woman is recruited to play the hero's sidekick, his prize, the villain's victim, or all three, passively aiding and abetting the hero-centric narrative. Her idealised form is the pristine maiden who, helpless, pure, and innocent of any violence, waits for the man to save and claim her as his right. Not unusually, she is reduced to a decorative backdrop for the men's glorified rutting. She is all but nameless, a truly sleeping beauty. Who remembers what she was called in *Spiderman*, *Captain America*, *Thor*, or any James Bond film?

Efforts to switch a woman into the hero role often fail dramatically because the quest she is expected to undergo remains a traditionally masculine, martial one; to succeed she has to act at being a man and a violent one at that. In *GI Jane*, Demi Moore's character is secretly allowed to train for a special forces role normally off-limits to women. Her male peers reject her as inferior until, after relentless baiting, she shaves her head; when her instructor beats her up, she head-butts him and yells 'Suck my dick!' Only then do her fellow trainees cheer and finally accept her as one of their own. This film and others like it are presented as showcases for the empowerment of women, but the only way Moore's character could succeed in her own story, according to the film's conceit, was to ape a man.

Similar problems plagued the ill-conceived attempt to reboot *Superman* as *Supergirl*, which has a young heroine of superhuman strength defeating monsters and villains without so much as bending a knee. Its star, Helen Slater, ruefully reflected years later: '[S]omething about having a girl superhero needs to be different from a super man.'[118] Hollywood's film-makers, mostly alpha males, appear to think that a heroine should do whatever a hero does – destroy the villain by violence – while wearing as little as possible for the duration. It is as if there were no route to salvation other than by way of the hyper-masculine hero, whether played by a man or a woman.

For all the superficial appeal of the stock, square-jawed male hero to adolescent boys, he would be a sorry, stunted soul in real life. While appearing to master his gender contradictions, he has only imposed an unimaginative, regimental order on them. By disavowing as weak the traits associated with the feminine or the non-heterosexual masculine, he has lost the subtleties of character that make for a compelling personality. Crises of grief, fear, or conscientious doubt – all hallmarks of a genuinely rich humanity – are off-limits to the traditional action hero, just as they are also suppressed in the real-life military. The schlocky hero character is a cardboard study in mediocrity and gender conformity, impotent beyond his narrow martial role and lost without a dystopian world to throw himself against. In being less of a person than a person, he is also less of a man than a man, as trapped in his own hyper-masculinity as he is enabled by it. James Bond would not know what to do if the woman he fancied felt nothing for him or pre-empted him by defeating the villain herself, because the traditional martial hero cannot step out of his role, nor does he share it, nor is he second to anyone else.

As adults, we might well smirk knowingly at the predictable devices of the action film, but adolescent boys are less resilient, more likely to find the hero's allure beguiling. As such, Hollywood grants the armed forces a bridgehead into the fantasy lives of young people, especially when the hero has an explicitly military role. In essence, recruiters hope to convert Hollywood's arousing spectacle of heroic warfare into a compelling dream of military life in the real world. Research on British infantry recruits found that war films were among the main influences on their decision to enlist.[119] Whereas older recruits were more likely to dismiss Hollywood as unrealistic, the younger thought the films promised a positive experience of army life. 'They're great,' said a trainee in the Yorkshire Regiment, 'they just make you want to get out there and get involved.'[120]

When *Top Gun* was released in 1986, US Navy recruiters set up stalls in cinemas across the country; sales of aviator shades leapt, as did applications to enlist.[121] Evidently, teens wanted to follow after Tom Cruise's alpha-male character, Maverick, in whose phallocentric world of top guns a bar becomes 'a target-rich environment' of single women.[122] From time to time, recruiters have cannibalised Hollywood films to spin military careers to guileless youth. In 2011, scenes from *X-Men: First Class* were spliced into a US army recruiting ad, for example, suggesting preposterous parallels between soldiers and the film's sci-fi mutants. Earlier, in 2001, the wildly far-fetched *Behind Enemy Lines* was used in the same way for the US Navy, which asked: 'Wish they would make a movie about your job?'[123]

Recruiters are happy for young people at the movies to swallow an appealing *myth* – in both senses of the word – about military life, for it is so much more persuasive than the reality. A realistic movie about the average soldier's experience might make it as a psychological drama, but not an action-adventure. War scenes depicted by Hollywood as staple fare, such as clandestine incursions behind enemy lines, are almost unheard of in actuality. Even in a war zone such as Afghanistan, most personnel are moving stores, patrolling, or just waiting to be told what to do next. By definition, the martial hero of fantasy must be free to make his own choices, but the real-life military represents the very opposite of spirited independence. Training is designed to break down the recruit's civilian identity and mould him or her into a combatant, part of a war machine, unhesitatingly obedient to orders. The military has no place for mavericks, who are punished. Even *Saving Private Ryan*, which depicts ostensibly ordinary soldiers, still required them to be on a special mission away from the usual regime of control and routine.

The villain and the violence

The questing hero appeals to young people for another reason: however testing his world may be, it is reassuringly simple for the psyche to manage. He stands like an island of utopian order in a sea of chaos populated by fishy characters whose plain evil is beyond the pale and their anonymous minions: storm-troopers, orcs, and random, unshaven men.

The villain is a turn-on, for he excites our hope of exacting delicious revenge for his outrages. He must be destroyed or at least pushed back through whatever hole he came in by. In real life, negotiation with violent others is a perennial option, but the Hollywood villain must not be humane or reachable by any power other than violence. As the poet Ted Hughes wrote of our fantasy villains, it is '[as] if we should deny an enemy, rather than pin him down in everlasting negotiations'.[124] The more narrowly the script-writer draws the villain – that is, the more immutably evil he appears to be – the more that extreme violence is touted as the only viable means to overcome him. The only way to stop a completely evil, completely powerful, completely irredeemable villain is apparently to kill him, preferably spectacularly and at length.

The last thing a Hollywood film needs is a negotiated settlement in the first half-hour, or its audience doubting the justice of the hero's violence, but we might at least wish our action hero to be more than a violence machine. Although the martial heroes of old – Odysseus or Sir Gawain, for example – had no qualms about violence, their principal heroic virtue was their wits. Today, the romance-quest of Hollywood or the Xbox prizes witless violence as the only means by which the story may be won. I have heard teenagers leaving the cinema exchanging at length on how deliciously gory a particular scene was, as if the film were nothing more than a showcase for violence, devoid of characters, plot or premise. Some films, such as *Pacific Rim* and *GI Joe*, really are just that.

As we have grown used to milder forms of fantasy violence, film-makers and videogame designers have climbed every mountain to augment, elaborate and prolong their phantasmagorical displays of characters violating one another. Yet the scintillating brutality of screen violence remains remarkably anaemic. In the videogame *Call of Duty*, which affects to recreate military scenarios realistically, enemy combatants fall over gracefully when shot, mutter an effete *ergh!* and fade from the screen as if they were never there. Nowhere but in real life do the dying weep, scream, plead for mercy, and thrash about in a slick of their own blood.

Whatever scruple the hero's brutality might offend in the spectator is skilfully outmanoeuvred by framing the violence as an act of justice. The villain has perpetrated such evil acts that we are shocked, morally scandalised into accepting the story's conceit. In psychoanalytic terms, the spectator's *super-ego* is sedated by the convincing illusion of a just cause, leaving the subconscious desires of the *id* to indulge themselves in vindictive fantasies of retribution. By the time the hero finally starts to prevail over the villain, we the spectators have long since been enrolled into supporting his cause. I have watched such scenes at the cinema and felt myself inwardly urging the hero on, wondering at my vengeful self as I have wanted him to smite down the villain on my behalf. With brutality and justice fused in the spectator's mind, the violence can reach orgiastic levels without conscientious complaint; as the violence peaks at the story's apex, so does our pleasure.

This is not to argue, whether for prudish or churlish reasons, for a blanket ban on all screen violence. A child's mind needs to range imaginatively over their world, including situations of conflict, in order to evaluate it aesthetically and morally. That journey of imagination probably ought to include fantasies of violence, provided that these are psychically held within – and evaluated against – the real-life experience of peace, meaning healthy relationships. But such a contained, contextualised presentation of screen violence is not the norm. The cultural dominance of the action-adventure film risks saturating the cultural imaginarium of young people with its morally framed, indulgent brutality. Children are bombarded with its core message: that violence is the necessary agent of redemption and progress, a staple choice rather than an aberrant failure of relationship to be lamented and confronted. Most children, especially boys, are groomed for fantastical violence from an early age, having soaked in the many hyper-violent cartoons on daytime television. By the time the adolescent boy encounters the martial heroes of films and videogames, the association of justice and righteous violence will already be entrenched as an acceptable idea.

Dolf Zillmann, a leading academic on the psychology of entertainment, wrote that the research 'projects nothing but ill effects from the thrills of violent entertainment'.[125] Studies have found repeatedly that screen violence increases the risk of committing violent behaviour.[126] Children are particularly vulnerable to these effects, especially boys of all ages and children of either gender aged 6–11.[127] Among the main risk factors are high exposure to screen violence, spectator identification with violent characters, and believing that the drama resembles real life.[128] A large US study found that boys with pre-existing aggressive behaviours were particularly affected by TV violence, but aggression also increased among those with no such history, indicating a generally deleterious effect of screen violence.[129] Framing violence as justice also appears to play a role; one study found that children who identified with aggressive heroes on screen tended to 'rehearse heroic and aggressive acts more'.[130] Socio-economic factors matter, too: under-achievement at school is associated with greater aggression, more frequent viewing of violent TV, and perceptions that screen violence is like real life.[131]

Given their higher consumption of violent, fantastical portrayals of the military and the effects these have on aggressive behaviour, it is unsurprising that young people from poor backgrounds become the primary enlistment pool for the armed forces.[132] Society's worries about youth violence on the streets are met with proposals to recruit more disaffected young people into the army, or introduce them to military discipline through cadet forces in the state education system. The government's hope, according to the academic Victoria Basham, is that the army's 'organised violence could be a substitute for disorganised violence' in communities.[133] The expectation that the army will transmute disaffection into heroism fits our warrior romance culture, but in reality, deployment to war zones substantially increases the risk that soldiers will behave violently when they come home.[134]

As the theologian Walter Wink has pointed out, we ought to be wary of the socio-cultural effects of repeated exposure to heroic martial fantasies.[135] They relentlessly inculcate the notion that violence is the one effective guarantor of peace; that when problems are difficult to solve yet morally urgent, violence can and must save the day. The proposition has no logic: the urgency of a problem has no bearing on what its effective solution might be. It also makes poor policy. The pragmatic use of violence is typically counter-productive in the cause of justice, whether the context is personal relationships or international relations. Teenagers' aggressive responses to interpersonal conflict are more often regarded as delinquent than rewarded as noble.[136] The British share of military interventions in Iraq, Afghanistan and Libya – all predicated on the redemptive power of violence after a professed failure of diplomacy – failed to bring a just peace. The idea that violence tends to work when all else fails is magical thinking: a wholly irrational construct built upon our passional fantasies of war, shaped and reinforced by the martial romance-quest that is so prevalent in our culture.

Personally speaking, I can appreciate the appeal of the warrior romance. It offers a fantasy of heightened reality: something more than the humdrum, everyday trudge of milky handed office workers with nothing to fight for, where nothing is at stake and our animal bodies go unused and atrophy. There is a sort of existential purity in imagining that life and death are compressed into the crucible of a single moment. A Falklands War veteran told me that being in the war was a sort of 'pure living':[137] all manner of things that matter little, like last night's TV, house prices, mid-season sales and so on, are in their proper place, far away, mattering little. But his 'pure living' was also the business of mass killing. He hated being immersed in the base, kill-or-be-killed violence of the war and later said he would counsel any young person against enlistment. We might vicariously enjoy the heroic warfare of the Hollywood romance-quest, but its counterpart in life has real people tearing each other apart.

Moral order, political order

It is easy to imagine that the romance-quest is defined by the entertaining battle between hero and villain, but these are merely the players that strut and fret upon the stage. The essence of the drama concerns the threatened, then restored, order of the world; it piques our attention by invoking our primal anxiety to preserve what we perceive as familiar order from what we perceive as threatening chaos. At this level, the drama begins when the disruption of order provokes uneasiness and uncertainty in the spectator. It continues in this state of tension, which energises the narrative. When order is finally restored, our anxiety resolves into satisfaction, uncertainty into assurance. We can relax and the film can end, perhaps with some intimation that we will go through all this again in the sequel.

The ritualised, to-and-fro pagan struggle between summer and winter, as described by Northrop Frye, was preoccupied with order of a different kind. In that drama, the earth's dynamic equilibrium was perennially at stake. Its continuing health depended on the diligent, ritual attentiveness of the tribe, whose lives depended in turn on the ecological order. By enacting and embodying the seasonal procession, the people ritualised their ecological belonging. Again, this is all lost on the stock Hollywood romance-quest, which venerates a geopolitical order represented by the prevailing imperial power, namely America and its coterie of Western states. This is gratingly patent in overtly nationalistic fare like *Captain America*, *GI Joe*, and *Independence Day*, but *Batman*'s Gotham and *Star Trek*'s Federation of Planets are, like the home-worlds of most Hollywood films, merely stand-ins for American nationhood. Whereas the pagan ritual drama ensured survival by preserving the earth, the Hollywood film achieves the same by preserving America.

Our post-modern age may be suspicious of the ideological grand narrative, but this is precisely what Hollywood lends the political order of the day. By fusing moral necessity with state power – which is to say, imperial American power – the modern romance-quest enthrones the American state at the heart of the world's proper order. Consequently, with his fight for justice aligned with a fight for his state, the hero becomes a patriot, his quest a nationalist one; his readiness to end his enemies with violence corresponds conveniently with the political outlook of his state. Across the water, a less-than-human, fearsome version of 'otherness' is laid over jaundiced fantasies of Germany, Russia, and now Islam, each represented by villains with sinister accents and exotic clothing in dark hues.

Once the Hollywood film has aligned the moral order of the world with the American state and enrolled the hero as its defender, his role as the people's champion must be reined in, his passion for justice pruned back. The initial episodes of the *Superman* radio series in 1940 introduced him as 'a champion of equal rights… fighter against the forces of hate and prejudice and for truth and justice'.[138] By the time of the 'Red Scare' McCarthy era in the 1950s, the TV series had him fighting 'for truth, justice and the American way', all references to civil rights and equality quietly dropped.[139] The superhero could not be the hired gun of the prevailing economic and political system and also an unaffiliated servant of universal equality. In Superman's latest adventure, *Man of Steel*, he is reduced to a glorified soldier of the global superpower. Unable to defeat his enemy alone, he combines his super-strength with the might of the US military to save Earth in a succession of drawn-out battles with scowling super-villains. A number of other sci-fi films, such as *Independence Day* and *Godzilla*, have similarly turned to the US military to save the planet for us.

Whilst many Hollywood films appear to reverse the structure of the romance-quest by presenting corrupt states that the hero fights against, usually these dystopian governments are carefully drawn so as not to resemble America. The *Star Wars* saga and the *Total Recall* remake are examples of politically safe imagined rebellions against imperial power. In contrast, films depicting villainous states that look a little like America risk antagonising the corporate oligarchs who own the entertainment industry. This might explain the premature demise of the TV space-western series *Firefly*, whose heroic band of space-faring bootleggers dodged and thwarted an oppressive empire based on an imagined future Sino-American alliance. The show's premise turned the traditional romance-quest on its head by counterposing human freedom and America-like imperial power. The show's owners, the right-leaning Fox Network, seemed bent on seeing it die, first giving it a graveyard slot in its programming and then rueing its poor ratings. *Firefly* failed to roll over by itself, though. Its strong characters and watchable stories attracted nearly five million viewers per episode and a rabidly devoted cult following, who were stunned to see the successful show axed after the first few episodes had aired. Fox's *24*, by contrast, has so far put its ageing hero through nine series of plot-straining, vapid battles for the American state.

Most of the time, producers and the corporations that pay them stay on message. In order to keep things that way, Washington extends a long arm into Hollywood. To aid producers to make the films it likes, the Pentagon loans military hardware from rifles to fighter jets to aircraft carriers, provides technical advisors, and even sends troops to stand in as extras. On occasion, troops even star, as they did in *Act of Valor*, a US special forces showcase awkwardly shoehorned into a film. In return for this taxpayer-funded help, film-makers sign a contract promising that the production will 'help Armed Forces' recruiting and retention programs'.[140] A special office in Washington is even allowed to doctor the script; *Top Gun* was supposed to show a navy war plane crashing into its carrier, for example, but the Pentagon made sure that never happened.[141] Philip Strub, Special Assistant for the Entertainment Industry at the Pentagon, explains:

> 'We sign a contract with the film-makers, and the contract says, essentially, "We're going to give you… this equipment on these days based on this particular version of the script and you will show us edited

sequences as we go along just to see if in general it conforms to what we agreed on."[142]

For producers like Jerry Bruckheimer, who churns out patriotic, history-bending kitsch like *Top Gun*, *Pearl Harbour* and *Black Hawk Down*, the arrangement is ideal. Those who look askance at US policy face the dilemma of either hiring military hardware at prohibitive cost, or allowing the state to dictate parts of the script. Films that show soldiers going feral or wracked with moral doubts, or which satirise war, are not approved. *Full Metal Jacket*, *Apocalypse Now*, *Thin Red Line*, *Platoon* and *Three Kings* all had to source military matériel from elsewhere. [143] Even films that lionise US forces are denied support if they portray scenarios at odds with current policy, such as *GI Jane*, in which a woman completes special forces training.[144]

Humanity's richer hope – peace with justice for all – privileges no one and no state; it is an ecology of flourishing, mutual relationships between peoples and with the earth. In peace, structures of power like governments serve the whole, not only themselves. Next to this, the imperial, warlike *Pax Americana* that Hollywood prefers is particularly shallow and faithless. While film-makers style their own state as a beacon of freedom shining into the dingy stupor of a disordered world, the real world gazes back at an overweening empire with a myopic squint, unable to see even itself with any clarity.

Nevertheless, the tacit political rhetoric of the typical Hollywood film performs a powerful psychological and cultural function in the service of the state. Part of Hollywood's appeal is in showing us real-world challenges as we would prefer to see them: villains in far-away places who spoil the proper ordering of the world until we bring them down. Who are these villains and how are they made in real life? For years while Saddam Hussein and the Afghan Taliban were oppressing ordinary people, Western governments were supporting them politically and financially.[145] General Galtieri invaded and then defended the Falkland Islands almost entirely by the strength of naval and military matériel that Britain, France and the US had sold him.[146] Today, Saudi Arabia, a monarchical dictatorship that severely oppresses women and suppresses political dissent, benefits from British arms worth billions of pounds through deals known to have been corrupt,[147] but which David Cameron still describes as 'legitimate and right'.[148] The major sponsor of the high-class Poppy Ball during the annual Armistice commemoration, BAE Systems, is also the main British-based supplier of Saudi's weapons.[149] Hollywood's maverick psychopath comes out of the blue to threaten us; in the real world, we often helped to make him long before the war began.

Whatever the world's proper order is held to be, the tinpot despot or suicide bomber is not what threatens it most. The deepening fissures in our humanity and our ecology are the logical outcome of a global economic system that generates billionaires and paupers, marginalises democracy, and arms dictators whom it first welcomes as friends and later condemns as enemies. The major insecurities we face as a country and as a species have systemic, historic roots, of which the madcap choices of despots are merely the expected symptomatic effects. Hence, our global turpitude has less to do with the demented villain that the hero fights to defeat than it has with the system that he fights to preserve. After all, when Batman is not chasing criminals through the slums of Gotham, he is the billionaire tycoon, Bruce Wayne, figurehead of the 1% in whose shadow the slums spread out.

The typical romance-quest also reinforces a tidy but bogus fantasy about our history, in which, from time to time, a villain launches a war against us, we win it, and peace is restored. In reality, war belongs to the process of history, is largely beyond the control of the belligerents once it has started, and has no discrete endpoint. The imperial rivalries of the 19th Century set the stage for the First World War, which set the stage for the Second World War, which set the stage for the Cold War, which set the stage for the wars in Vietnam, Iraq, the former Yugoslavia, Afghanistan and elsewhere. Rather than discrete events which, like stories, have neat beginnings, middles and endings, the world's wars shade into one another; they are the traumatic eternal return of a political and economic system which readily lends itself to armed conflict. The start of war is no longer formally declared; the end of war is, but typically prematurely. Our failure to recognise that war is a function of historical process keeps us in a state of endless warring, with Britain and the US first among industrialised nations to initiate the action.

The glossy war of Hollywood has helped to reignite the warrior romance in Western culture and recover the image of the US military after its shaming in Vietnam, but culture can also depict Western governments in a gloomier, dystopian light, and we like that, too. It vexes the Pentagon that few people over the age of 21 would prefer *Top Gun* to *Apocalypse Now*, which often tops Best War Movie lists along with other films free from Pentagon interference, such as The *Thin Red Line*, *The Deer Hunter* and *Three Kings*.[150] Even so, recruiters will not mind too much as long as the teen market and its future soldiers still want to be the latest incarnation of Maverick.

The romance-quest and the politics of war

However politically implausible the traditional romance-quest may be, its power to shape how Western states frame their geopolitical outlook is remarkable. Consider how closely the US and UK policy on the Iraq War conformed to a romance-quest. The war was characterised as the democratic West heroically removing the villainous Saddam Hussein in order to liberate a country and preserve order globally. The story has the hero, the villain, the violence, and the restored moral order, but becomes outlandish when the war is considered in its historical context. Iraq was part of the British Empire after the First World War; popular rebellion was put down by British air power against civilians in the 1920s; Britain left Iraq in a political mess, but continued to extract its oil through British Petroleum. Through this mire, Saddam rose to power and the West armed and supported him. His chemical attack on the people of Halabja in 1988, which killed 5,000 civilians, was carried out using hardware sold to him by Western corporations with their governments' blessing.[151] The US-led invasion in 2003 was opposed by the United Nations and also, apparently, by most of the world's population including Iraqis. The action removed Saddam Hussein but it led to more than 120,000 verified Iraqi dead, mostly civilians.[152] Iraq's future remains in the balance; in 2013, nearly 10,000 people were killed in the continuing insurgency.[153]

Many other summaries are possible, but any historically sensitive analysis will show how ill-fitting are the terms of a romance-quest. Who is the hero, who the villain? How redemptive is violence that results in so many dead women and children? Whose moral order was disturbed, whose restored? And why are the people of Iraq facing chaos daily, so long after the war's end?

Yet the UK and US did treat the war in the manner of a romance-quest. On 1 May 2003, President Bush was flown aboard the *USS Abraham Lincoln* in a military jet and, still wearing his combat flight gear, was fêted on the deck as a conquering hero. He could have been an ageing version of *Top Gun*'s Maverick or Harrison Ford's hard-boiled President in *Air Force One*. The media made much of his jet's call sign, *Navy One*, as if he might fly a few missions himself; it is now on display in the US National Aviation Museum as the President's own war plane. A plastic-toy maker even created a new heroic figure of the President as a combat aviator.

From the deck of the aircraft carrier, but changed into presidential attire, Bush gave what resembled an end-of-film speech: 'In the battle of Iraq, the United States and her allies have prevailed,' he declared.[154] Referring to US troops killed in the war to date, he rhapsodised:

> 'Those we lost were last seen on duty. Their final act on this earth was to fight a great evil and bring liberty to others. All of you – all in this generation of our military – have taken up the highest calling of history. You're defending your country, and protecting the innocent from harm. And wherever you go, you carry a message of hope – a message that is ancient and ever new. In the words of the prophet Isaiah, "To the captives, *come out*, – and to those in darkness, *be free*."'[155]

He did not mention the 'great evil' by name, for Saddam was still hiding out. Although the ousted leader could have had no further role in the war, he was still the fantasy villain in a romance-quest, so prodigious efforts were being made to find and finish him.

It turned out that the war had yet to finish, too, but two months later, still celebrating the false dawn of success, Tony Blair was invited to address both Houses of Congress and receive the Congressional Gold Medal – America's answer to knighthood. If George W Bush's speech brought one romance-quest to an end, Tony Blair's encouraged him to make a sequel. 'Our new world rests on order,' he said; 'the danger is disorder.'[156] His speech led his audience on a round-the-world recce of problems the West faced and their solutions. He cautioned briefly that insecurity has systemic roots – a message Washington never likes to hear – but his main purpose was to egg the US on as the rightful heir to global empire, problem-solver to the world. The speech's well-crafted oratory left Congress in states of rapture; its romantic, ingratiating tone was no less gushing than the President's had been: '[W]hat you bequeath to this anxious world is the light of liberty,' our Prime Minister said.[157] He addressed the US as if it had invented freedom and owned its patent – as if its globalised corporate capitalism had nothing to do with Bangladeshi sweatshops, propped-up dictators in Latin America and Africa, or an overheating planet. To repeated cheers and standing ovations, Tony Blair gave Americans the message of which only heroes are worthy: 'Destiny put you in this place in history and the task is yours to do.'

Tony Blair and George W Bush were telling the preferred story of empire, which is its own romance-quest: the mandate of heaven is ours; our cause is just; it falls to us to defeat evil. Both speeches traded on age-old colonial presumptions: the oppressed do not bring peace through their own efforts; peace is brought to them by the heroic actions of world powers. Nor do the downtrodden free themselves through solidarity with others; they are liberated by the decisions of men in suits who 'prevail' and then slap themselves on the back. Such stupefying rhetoric screens out the genesis of suffering in the dominant systems of the world, which are hierarchical, patriarchal and divisive.

Messing with the story

Under the sheer cultural weight of the hyper-masculine saviour figure, what alternative fantasies might aid young people to meet their needs for authenticity, belonging and effective personal power, while presenting a less predictable world of richer possibilities? This might seem unlikely beyond rarefied, artsy fare, but the romance-quest of popular culture has always produced a minority of heroic role-model characters who creatively make a mess of the rules. Among recent mainstream teen movies that have tried to do this, it is worth looking at three: *Avatar, The Hunger Games* and *Ender's Game*. All three films are based on a warrior hero's quest but all push against its conventions to subvert the genre. At their best, these films ask apt political questions of their audience: Who or what is the real enemy, if there is one at all? What is the proper order of the world and who gets to decide? Who benefits from the state's story of the world? How redemptive is violence in the cause of justice, and what alternatives does the hero have?

In *Avatar*, US marine Jake Sully is posted to the planet Pandora, where a mining project for a mineral needed on Earth is suffering terrorist attacks from the native primitive aliens; his orders are to infiltrate their tribe and gather intelligence for a major offensive. The film starts as a romance-quest in the spaghetti western mould: civilised European pioneers set out to conquer savage native Americans, bringing God, order, and prosperity. While living with the Pandorans, however, Jake begins to share their wonder for their living home and soak in the cultural wealth of their simple society. The forest becomes mesmerisingly beautiful to him, while the aliens' generosity of spirit begins to embarrass his faith in his military employers, whom he now sees as stooges in hock to the mining corporation. The company of the Pandorans and their wild, vulnerable forest brings healing to the battle-hardened, battle-damaged marine, as if the forest's presence were its own reproach to the imperial order for which Jake was sent to fight. Dispatched as the hero to impose order on an alien world, his encounter surprises by giving him back his self and turning his allegiance about.

Notwithstanding the romanticisation of the 'noble savage', the film's first half compellingly presents wonder and communion, and not violence, as the redemptive activities at the heart of the narrative. This part of the film breaks down the hero and villain roles, displaces the presumption to violence, and reverses assumptions about the moral order that needs restoring. Disappointingly, the film's conclusion collapses into a run-of-the-mill James Cameron action movie. The story is won by means that its very premise is meant to question, namely prolonged, mass violence, as if the Indians just killed all the cowboys and called it poetic justice.

The romance-quest of *Avatar* switches roles and raises questions, but never departs from the belief that moral order is only restored when a hero violently prevails over his villain. In *The Hunger Games*, the 'real enemy' is not a character, but the state-sponsored spectacle of violence itself. The film's action is set in the fictional world of Panem, a dictatorship of 12 segregated, tightly controlled districts ruled by an opulent capitol. In District 12, the poorest of Panem's people starve as they work the mines and suffer the sadistic whims of Panem's militarised police. In the Capitol, the élite enjoy the high life of their bountiful, ordered world. To control society fully and glorify its victory over a failed popular rebellion, every year the Capitol forces two children from each of the 12 districts to fight to the death in a spectacular reality TV show. These 'Hunger Games' are spun as 'a pageant of honour, courage and sacrifice' to remind the world that 'freedom has a cost'. Far from rebelling against the Games, the people of the divided districts take to the spectacle as 'something that knits us all together' and they devour the action on huge public screens.

The heroine, Katniss, and her fellow tribute, Peeta, are nominated to fight for District 12. Loath to kill, they are nonetheless haplessly coerced into violence and eventually win through together by grit, wit and luck, but the Games require a lone winner; one will have to kill the other. Apparently cornered by the violent system, Katniss and Peeta nonetheless refuse its expectation, resolving instead to poison themselves while the whole world watches. At the last minute, the government panics and declares them jointly victorious. The Capitol's near-total power of control, represented entirely by men, has faltered, creating a moment of awakening for the poorest of Panem who take to Katniss as a champion of revolutionary hope. The aspirational world of the casually unconcerned super-rich – the Capitol's 'crystal chandeliers, platinum doorknobs' – is betrayed for what it is: a sham built on injustice and violence.

The story cleverly reorders the conventional romance-quest. Katniss is stoical, strong, resolute, ready to use violence if she has to – in these ways a typical martial hero – but she is also generous, often afraid, and knows she relies on others as they rely on her. The film's treatment of violence also subverts the genre. In such a state of complete coercion, the hero's violence would appear to be the only viable redemptive power, but only when Katniss and Peeta refuse the use of violence do they outwit the government's violence and weaken its hold on the people.

The story's creator, Suzanne Collins, explains the genesis of her idea:

> 'I was channel surfing between reality TV programming and actual war coverage when Katniss's story came to me. One night I'm sitting there flipping around and on one channel there's a group of young people competing for, I don't know, money maybe? And on the next, there's a group of young people fighting an actual war. And I was tired, and the lines began to blur in this very unsettling way, and I thought of this story.'[158]

Collins explains that the film is a modern re-imagining of the Theseus and Minotaur myth, in which Crete periodically demands 14 child tributes from Athens as retribution for a past crime. The children are thrown into a labyrinth where the half-man, half-bull Minotaur devours them, until one year Theseus takes a child's place and slays the monster. The world of Panem combines numerous references to ancient Roman and modern American culture. Panem, for example, from *panem et circenses*, was the condition of 'bread and circuses' by which the Roman state kept its citizens complacent and politically docile. This historical idea is translated to a modern-day fictional setting of riot police, economic injustice, and TV game shows. The 'Capitol' was originally the precinct of the Temple of Jupiter in ancient Rome, but is better known today as the seat of the US legislature. Panem, as a hybrid of ancient Roman and modern American cultures, lends the film a prophetic air, asking questions of its audience, as prophecies do, about the kind of future we want our children to know.

One of the most imaginatively subversive mainstream action-adventure films in recent times has been another sci-fi offering, *Ender's Game*, which, like *The Hunger Games*, also features warrior children who question the violent norms of the adult world. In the future, Earth is threatened to the point of destruction by an alien invasion, which is only just fought off at the eleventh hour. Years later, the aliens are re-arming at an exponential rate; a pre-emptive strike against their home planet is humankind's only chance of survival. By this point, the evolution of videogames has created a generation of preternaturally talented teens with such lightning reactions and strategic prowess that they alone are capable of remotely controlling Earth's massive fleet of space drones. These teen soldiers will orchestrate the attack.

Earth's military commanders – American, of course – have invested all their hope in a young gamer of unusual gifts and maturity, the oddly-named Ender Wiggin. The problem is that Ender has no heroic ambition, is profoundly wary of violence, and is too free-thinking for the regimentation of his military training. Ender knows his own power, is even afraid of it, and cannot help but empathise with those who oppose him:

> 'I've had a lot of fights... I've won because I've always understood the way my enemy thinks and when I truly understand them [I] also love them. I think it's

impossible to truly understand someone and not love
them the way they love themselves but in that
moment... I destroy them. I make it impossible for them
ever to hurt me again.'

When given the command of a squadron of fellow teen warrior-gamers, he subverts military convention by telling them they will lead together and learn from each other, which wins their trust. When he fights off a bully, he is ashamed of his violence – still more so that he found it satisfying. He learns to reason with other bullies by respecting them while standing his own ground, searching hard for a win-win outcome. His vivid dreams about the enemy alien race intrigue and trouble him; he is curious about their exotic anatomy and wonders what it is like to think like they do.

Ender's squadron undergoes a series of simulated remote-control space battles in preparation for war, culminating in the spectacular annihilation of the aliens' planet. When Ender is told that he was tricked – the massacre was real after all – he is hysterically distraught that he has just committed genocide. Worse, he realises now that the aliens were not aggressing; their motive for re-armament was the same as Earth's – fear of attack. As Earth celebrates its victory, Ender finds a single alien egg and sets off to find it a home on another planet to atone for his crime.

Throughout the film, Ender is fully himself, a whole person, not just a hero. This is why the military need him, but also why they cannot control him. He alone suspects that the unknowable, alien other is not the existential threat that his commanders suspect, even if he learns the truth too late. Ender demonstrates to adolescent viewers, and indeed to the rest of us, that our tendency to leap to violence is a vice, not a virtue, and has nothing to do with what makes a person genuinely interesting or effective in the world. The film subverts every other component of the romance-quest, too. The hero refuses to be a hero; the villain is not really the villain; the violence that first appears to be redemptive turns out to be criminal; and the moral order of the world is at odds with the diktats of the prevailing empire. At the same time, Ender is a compelling figure, and the true redemptive power in the story is his connection with the 'humanity' of the alien other.

Unlike the stock Hollywood action hero, we can imagine Jake, Katniss and Ender leading meaningful lives after their quests have ended. Not only are their characters richer than usual, so are the worlds they move in. They are complex enough, at least, to allow the life of a forest or an alien other to draw out the humanity of the warrior hero and lead them to question the role they are made to perform. Compared with the usual linear, straitjacketed Hollywood action-adventure story, these films' narratives are more open, more ecological in the broad sense of 'ecology' meaning an environment of responsive relationships. Once the lead character has cracked open the martial hero role to find a real person within, the story may be shaped by any number of choices, of which violence is only one. Through these alternative possibilities, the hero fills out as a character, as do we as his or her spectator-supporters. The war-or-weakness presumption is debunked.

These films are neither politically radical nor non-violent, but they do offer a mass audience a partial counter-narrative to the prevailing political order. All three films portray a dominant, America-like state wielding the power of empire. In each case, that state is wrapped in its own rhetoric of worldly beneficence, yet is complacent in its self-image, eager to use military power, afraid of dissent, and anxious to control its world to the point of total dominance. Jake, Katniss and Ender are co-opted as the empire's pawns and enrolled into its self-justifying narrative, but their heroic, freedom-giving action is to resist it, expose it, disrupt it, and subvert it. In this way, each story shifts us from imagining the imperial state as the institution that defends justice and freedom, to realising that its primary purpose is to exercise control and enforce it through military violence. Tony Blair said in 2003 that the 'new world rests on order', alluding to the order imposed on Iraq by his choice to invade it.[159] The heroes of these films invite the possibility that freedom, justice and peace depend on the opposite: the creative disordering of the political consensus.

Avatar, The Hunger Games and *Ender's Game* are high-grossing, mainstream, romantic teen movies with mass appeal and an essentially hopeful outlook. They show that Hollywood has no good commercial reason to limit its churnings-out to the flag-coddled emptiness of *Olympus has Fallen* or the America-saved-history pretensions of *Behind Enemy Lines* – unless the world's most powerful cultural centre wants, as it seems, to persist with one eye on Washington, the other closed.

Screened

While in Afghanistan, Prince Harry likened firing the weapons of his Apache helicopter to the pleasure of a game:

> '[It's a] joy for me because I'm one of those people that love playing Playstation and Xbox, so with my thumbs I like to think that I'm probably quite useful. You can ask the guys, I thrash them at Fifa the whole time.' [160]

Among those who criticised the Prince's comments was a Taliban spokesman, who accused him of being remote from direct fighting and reducing war to a game, [161] but perhaps peering into the aircraft's instruments in the middle of the night, aligning blips on a screen, and pressing the red button does feel like a game. After all, 3D videogame technology was originally developed for military use. Cruise missiles were launched into Iraq from screens in the dark bellies of ships hundreds of miles away. From Nevada and now Lincolnshire, drone pilots guide missiles to targets in Afghanistan some thousands of miles distant. This is real war, but experienced unreally – that is, on screens, virtually. The screen war of a videogame may be no less convincing an experience than a real war represented on the screen of an Apache – *convincing* insofar as the player can make believe that they are in a war, but not *realistic*, for no one gets their face shot off.

The Hollywood action film can offer a fantasy of spectating at a war; the videogame promotes us to fantasy participants. Conversely, war itself can be made to appear like a videogame, such as when the visual feed from a guided bomb is piped through to living room TVs. Hence, videogame representations of hi-tech warfare begin to resemble our distanced fantasy of the real thing. As a thought experiment, imagine a dark room with two screens on opposite walls. One displays the visual feed from a drone as seen by its remote pilot; the other shows scenes from a videogame which aims to present a convincing spectacle of drone warfare. An observer could probably tell the difference between the real war and the unreal war today, but perhaps not in a decade's time. The experiences of the respective operators, on the other hand – the drone pilot and the gamer – would still be worlds apart.

The latest games show near-photo-realistic graphics in first-person perspective. Bullets whizz past or bounce off the virtual avatar of the mesmerised player, who tears through a swarm of nameless foes with nothing but his hyper-vigilant thumbs. The appeal to a young mind craving a feeling of power is obvious; *Call of Duty's* latest instalments are called 'Onslaught' and 'Devastation', with the player-protagonist as usual at the heart of the spectacle.

Game designers swaddle their orgiastic virtual killing in pretensions to realism and contemporary relevance. *Medal of Honor: Warfighter*, claiming to be 'inspired by real-world threats', is one of many examples.[162] Drawing on advice from well-paid veterans, the game promises to '[put] gamers in the boots of today's most precise and disciplined warrior' on the hunt for Osama Bin Laden, and show them what 'the fight against the ongoing global terror threat 'is really like.[163] The game ties in its story with the film *Zero Dark Thirty* and uses real-world maps of Pakistan – the only real thing about it.[164]

Kuma's so-called episodic games go one better by allowing gamers to participate vicariously in re-imagined contemporary conflicts even as they are happening. The developers of *Kuma War* package details from the news into up-to-the-minute war missions, sending 'multiple updates monthly to the consumer's computer to reflect unfolding events in the real world'.[165] In effect, Kuma invites you to fight the war you are watching on the news.

When Kuma designed a mission to storm the nuclear plant at Natanz in Iran, an Iranian student group retaliated with its own game, in which their troops break into US and Israeli strongholds to rescue a kidnapped nuclear scientist and his wife.[166] 'This is our defence against the enemy's cultural onslaught,' the group said.[167]

China has produced *Glorious Revolution* for gamers to gun down US troops and aircraft, and which the People's Liberation Army now use to train new recruits.[168] It is a brazen exercise in ideological indoctrination, but that is probably what the people of China would make of *Virtual Battlespace 2*, the British army's training game for soldiers in which they practise storming insurgent strongholds in Asia. The training game is an adapted version of the commercial shoot-'em-up, *Armed Assault*, programmed for scenarios in Afghanistan.[169] A freely downloadable variant with Ministry of Defence branding was designed for recruiters to hand out as a freebie for young people asking what the army is like.[170]

The only genuine battleground in these games is the mind of the child who plays them. In that psychological arena, videogame designers, with their government's blessing, compete to impose an ideological story of nationalist kitsch about their world. The political stripe of the games varies superficially according to their country of origin, but all reduce contemporary geopolitics to a zombie shoot-'em-up fantasy for screen-hypnotised gamers. Before long, every state with imperial ambitions will have its own virtual, nearly-indestructible warrior champion slaying hordes of foreigners on a warped world map with itself at the centre. The games will help to ensure that children the world over love their own state, whichever it may be, and joyfully approve of its enmities.

A few developers have tried to break the mould with commercially viable games that present contemporary geopolitics as a complex dystopia. *Spec Ops – The Line* is 'a game that makes you feel bad', according to Ole Reissmann of *Spiegel Online*,[171] but it is also popular. The format brings the punters in with the usual marriage of techno-fetish and bloodbath, but its narrative goes horribly wrong, confronting the player's participation in it. Michael Schulze von Glasser, who has researched the on-screen warfare of the gaming world, says that the game's designers were inspired by Conrad's *Heart of Darkness* and Coppola's *Apocalypse Now*:

> 'In *Spec Ops*, the gamer is the leader of a three-part US-reconnaissance troop that, in a fictitious near-future scenario, is despatched to Dubai, which has been destroyed by desert storms. In the city there are merciless skirmishes and shoot-outs involving civilians,

CIA agents, and US troops under the command of Colonel Konrad, who is meant to be evacuating people. … There is no "good-bad" formula. During some missions, Colonel Konrad's troops seem to abduct the civilians, during others they help them. Moreover, Konrad's soldiers fight against the CIA. The gamer's troop start off fighting alongside the secret service. However, in doing so they unintentionally eliminate the city's remaining water supplies.

'The gamer, with the help of two comrades, then fights his way towards Colonel Konrad's troops whose operations centre is located in a high-rise building in the city. The two comrades die in their pursuit: the streets of the ruined city are lined with countless (and at times decomposing) corpses. It is precisely these images which make *Spec Ops* such an extraordinary game: in one mission the gamer attacks enemy soldiers with phosphorous grenades, but sees how indiscriminate this weapon is when dozens of burning civilians then crawl towards them. The game's narrative is also very unusual: the gamer eventually learns that Colonel Konrad died some time ago and had suffered from a multiple personality disorder. Instead of successfully carrying out the mission of going to Dubai to observe what is happening and then leaving, the gamer and their two companions are drawn ever-closer to the conflict. The *Spec Ops* gamer justifies their own crimes by what Konrad has done before them. They are faced with multiple moral dilemmas: should they save a group of civilians, or a CIA agent who has crucial intelligence? Ultimately, in the crusade of *Spec Ops*, the gamer belongs to the bad side – despite the best intentions.

'*Spec Ops* is a challenge to the notion of "humanitarian military missions"; its chilling and at times unbearable images depict the horror of armed conflict.'[172]

The vast majority of output is still as callow as *Call of Duty*, but *Spec Ops* and some similar games demonstrate that popular entertainment can tell more than one story when it wants to; it need not ape the weary narrative of the righteous state prevailing over savage foreigners. When it does, however, the videogame's immersive spectacle of war provides recruiters with a new way to mine the fantasy lives of teens and turn them on to the prospect of military life.

At the largest videogame fair in the world, held in Cologne, armed forces recruiters set up stall. Heavy military hardware is parked up for gamers to clamber over while they puzzle out how it works, just as their digital alter-egos might do in a game. Michael Schulze von Glasser has been there. He says that visitors can play a war game inside a replica military helicopter, its windows replaced with virtual reality screens, while civvies paid to dress up as special forces soldiers brandish replica rifles and pose with gamers for photos.[173] Fantasy pursues reality; reality is camouflaged as fantasy. The two are so closely overlaid that the less-than-critical imagination melds them as one. For the younger intake of British soldiers, games like *Call of Duty* and *Gears of War* are among the main influences on their motives to enlist; they told researchers that firing guns was the best thing about the gameplay. 'It's great when you play a game and you get to use things like sniper rifles,' said an infantry trainee, 'that's what I want to do.'[174]

The US army was first to realise the recruitment potential of videogames, launching its own, *America's Army*, in 2002. The gameplay is inspired by a precursor to *Call of Duty* called *Counter-Strike*, which claims to present an 'incredibly realistic brand of terrorist warfare in [a] wildly popular team-based game'.[175] The latest *America's Army* scenario is played out in a fictional Central Asian country with a puppet government controlled by terrorists.[176] After the UN has failed to save civilian lives, the US has stepped in to take 'decisive action'.[177] This patriotically stylised version of the Afghanistan War has all the trappings of a Hollywood romance-quest: the requisite heroes and villains, plenty of violence, and the restitution of moral order to the glory of America.

To date, *America's Army* has benefited from $33 million of taxpayers' money, which has enabled recruiters to offer young people a state-of-the-art, free-to-download package while keeping an edge over the $60-or-so price tag of commercial games.[178] In essence, the gamer has a go at being a soldier on screen before clicking through to the recruiting site. If users have registered, which they are repeatedly encouraged to do, the game sends details of their performance to recruiters 'for the purpose of facilitating career placement within the Army'.[179] A recruiter then contacts the gamer to pitch the army's spiel.

America's Army tours the US as an immersive, virtual reality experience for use in schools and shopping malls. The *Digital Trends* website asked a US Air Force veteran, Bob, who was a keen gamer before enlisting, what he thought about this. '100 per cent bullshit,' he said:

> 'There are some recruitment stations where they've got big-time simulations set up. Four walls with projections, you're on a pretend jeep in combat. And it never crosses these kids' minds that it's not 110 degrees in there. You don't smell it. When your buddy gets shot, he doesn't scream the same way in a video game, you know?'[180]

The game's sanitised, glorified depiction of patriotic warfare is corny to the point of comical, but has nonetheless convinced thousands of American teens to enlist. According to the writer Nick Turse, *America's Army* has been more effective in marketing military life than all other US army communications combined, with around a third of young Americans aware of it.[181]

Evidently excited by the possibilities, the British army followed with its own recruitment game in 2009, aimed mainly at getting working-class teenagers to join the undermanned infantry.[182] A showcase video produced by the lead ad agency, Publicis, shows a sneering, hoodie stereotype giving the camera the finger, then fading to show the same lad in combat fatigues, smiling.[183] To attract the

Xbox generation, the agency 'had to talk to them in a language they understood', it said.[184] This meant distilling the appeal and style of hit games like *Call of Duty* to create a virtual experience that could win children's attention over the commercial competition.[185]

The ad agencies created *Start Thinking Soldier*, which combined computer graphics with first-person-perspective film footage of sanitised, mock war scenes filmed from a helmet camera. To film the scenes, the agencies flew out to Kenya and set up a tent city for 120 cast and crew outside the rural town of Magadi, where the landscape could be made to appear like Iraq or Afghanistan. A local bar was mocked up as a bomb factory, while an imitation nodding donkey turned the neighbouring salt flats (also seen in *The Constant Gardener*) into an oil field.[186] The extravagant production values pushed the cost of the project to twice the usual cost of an army recruitment campaign.[187] The result was a blend of documentary-style reportage with a videogame atmosphere – an 'immersive gaming recruitment experience' that was 'wholly believable', according to Katie Smith of Publicis.[188]

Players of *Start Thinking Soldier* were asked to make judgements about how to deal with angry locals or storm a building: kick the door in, blow a hole in the wall, call in an airstrike. 'What would you do?' was the game's tagline. As snipers, machine-gunners and mortar operators, British teens could have a go at 'neutralising' distant enemy positions to earn the congratulations of their voiced-over commander.

As with *America's Army*, users were invited to register their details when accessing *Start Thinking Soldier*. Their game performance was then sent to recruiters, who would 'start a dialogue with them', Katie Smith explained,[189] and gamers could click through to recruiters at any point for a live online chat. Special game features and access to the 'hi-score' leader-board were only offered to those who provided more personal details, which gave recruiters more contact options. The game also recommended specific army jobs to match the user's performance. I had a go at target-practice with my virtual SA-80 rifle and found I was a liability, shooting more than half of my bullets into the next field. 'You're a good shot', the game told me, 'with a

Top: girl band 'The Saturdays' open the British Legion Poppy Appeal with their song 'Notorious', 2013 (Photo: British Legion); middle-left: A C Gilbert Company's Hiroshima bomb game for American children, c. 1945-50; middle-right: Wyke Farms' Cheese for Heroes, 2013; bottom: extras posing as special forces soldiers with teenagers at the world's largest videogame fair, Gamescom, Cologne, 2012 (Photo: Michael Schulze von Glasser).

little more training you could even achieve marksman status.'[190]

The army still had to get their virtual recruits to meet real soldiers, so they invited the game's registrants to the *Start Thinking Soldier Experience*, a touring recruitment event for air shows and town fêtes that aimed to generate 'a conversation between soldiers and consumers'.[191] In virtual-reality-style army 'pods' made from converted shipping crates, children could try the *Start Thinking Soldier* missions: defusing bombs, driving tanks and firing at targets, each exercise introduced to a heavy rock soundtrack. A recruiter would meet the children as they left the pod, give them their game scores, hand them certificates, and tell them which parts of the army would suit them.

The British army spun *Start Thinking to Soldier* as a realistic portrayal of the army at war, but were there such a thing it would be in turns boring and gory. Soldiers mostly enjoy the army for the camaraderie of their mates, not the killing of warfare. War in *Start Thinking Soldier* is relentlessly exciting; gunfights are well ordered; no one is afraid; no civilians are hurt; nothing comes as a surprise. No one dies. The most common cause of death and injury among British forces in Afghanistan – the roadside bomb – only appears for the child gamer to disable it by virtually snipping its implausibly colour-coded wires.

Perhaps this picture of the army is wholly believable to a teenager, as Katie Smith suggests, but it is still a puffed-up fiction. One game scene showing soldiers giving out aid was so far-fetched that aid agencies complained in a joint letter to the Armed Forces Minister. The game painted 'a dehumanised picture' of the people receiving help, read the letter, and by depicting a military force as a distributor of aid, the concept showed a poor understanding of how relief work is carried out.[192]

The game was popular, though. According to the ad agencies, half a million people had a go at the first mission and 1.7 million people used the site during the campaign.[193] 80,000 users registered fully with their contact details – twice the target figure – and of these, more than a third said they intended to apply for an army job as a result of the game.[194] Helped along by the recession, the army met its recruitment targets for once, while the ad agencies won several industry gongs for integrating gaming and recruiting into a novel method of selling the army to the young.

The game was well conceived but was it really so successful in helping, as one of the marketing executives put it, to 'create people for the army'?[195] Curiously, in the year following the campaign the number of drop-outs among army trainees jumped,[196] corresponding approximately with those who would have applied to enlist while *Start Thinking Soldier* was online.[197] It could be a coincidence, but plausibly, house-bound gamers who warm to the army online like the real thing a lot less when their corporal starts balling at them to get up before the sun does. Perhaps it came as a shock to the campaign's recruits to discover that new infantrymen do not get to make judgement calls about how best to storm buildings; the soldier is conditioned by training to obey whatever orders are barked at him. And young gamers who are, as Prince Harry put it, useful with their thumbs, are of little use to the army unless they have also grown up jumping walls and swinging from trees. By presenting a believable gloss on infantry life to people who like to spend time indoors, *Start Thinking Soldier* could have been an expensively counter-productive recruitment strategy in the long run. We will never know, because the official evaluation of the £4.6 million project has mysteriously disappeared; the Ministry of Defence says it is 'no longer held'.[198] The army has since taken the full game offline and removed the links from its jobs site. Five years on, it has yet to look again at virtual reality as a recruitment tool, although its first recruitment game is unlikely to have been its last.[199]

Most important Chapter

CONTROL

'In this game the floor is the sea … We distribute our boards about the sea in an archipelagic manner. We then dress our islands … On the whole [the archipelago] is Indian in character – comprehensively Indian, east and west and Red Indian, as befits children of an imperial people … You see how the game goes on. We land and alter things, and build and rearrange, and hoist paper flags on pins, and subjugate populations, and confer all the blessings of civilisation upon these lands.'[200]

From 'The Game of Wonderful Islands' in *Floor Games* by H G Wells, 1913.

If peace is the ecology of mutual relationships, violence is the deliberate or negligent destruction of that ecology – the violation of persons, cultures, communities, peoples, the earth. As the theologian Isabel Carter Heyward puts it, violence is the negation of mutuality;[201] it denies a humane relationship with the other.

Control, as the will to force a situation into a specific outcome, or to prevent one, is one way of understanding the genesis of violence. Violent action in the home or neighbourhood, between peoples or nations, or against the earth, as well as its structured forms such as economic injustice, militarism, and ecocidal consumerism, all issue at some point from the will to control. That is, where there is violence, there is a corresponding attempt to forcibly manipulate the life of the world so as to benefit the sponsors of the violence. As such, violence is the extension of the will to control other beings; the will to control other beings culminates in violence.

One way of understanding empire is as the expansion and maintenance of control over others, such that the will to control, when writ large and successfully accomplished, achieves imperial dominance. Hence empire, unlike commonwealth, is a structure and process of violence, despite its chosen narrative of the righteous quest that professes to 'confer all the blessings of civilisation' upon the world.

Systems of violence are systems of control, and systems of control are by nature imperial. Those who participate in systems of violence, such as soldiers, are themselves controlled. The attempt to manufacture public support for war is another exercise in control. The controlled are dominated, which is to say that they are oppressed; they become, as the educationalist Paulo Freire expressed it, 'beings for another'.[202]

Such is the intimacy of violence, control and empire.

* * *

'Our country has always had global responsibilities and global ambitions,' runs the opening line of the government's defence posture document.[203] In order 'to reduce the likelihood of risks affecting the UK or our interests overseas', the state will apply 'all our instruments of power and influence to shape the global environment...'.[204] Despite criticisms of defence cuts from parliamentarians, the right-leaning press and the armed forces, the UK's military ambitions remains strong indeed. Ours is one of few states to retain a viable expeditionary capability, by which it can sustain a medium-sized war abroad. The huge expense of this policy makes the UK the sixth-largest military spender among the world's nearly 200 nations.[205]

Every new development now planned for the British military feeds one purpose: to enhance the capacity for projecting power worldwide.[206] There will be new aircraft carriers 'to deploy air power from anywhere in the world without the need for friendly air bases on land', and new helicopters to support amphibious landings.[207] New submarines will 'operate in secret across the world's oceans, fire Tomahawk cruise missiles at targets on land, detect and attack other submarines and ships to keep the sea lanes open'.[208] The 'reach and endurance' of new fighter jets and drones will be extended, and new heavy-lift aircraft will 'fly our forces wherever they are needed in the world'.[209] Following the lead of the United States, the UK will also expand its special forces for secret operations in far-away places.[210]

At the same time, the middle pages of the National Security Strategy quietly admit that from our backwater island realm 'we face no major state threat at present and no existential threat to our security, freedom or prosperity'.[211] So why is the British state attached to such a heavily militarised posture in relation to its world? The main reason given is to prevent a future atrocity inspired by al-Qa'ida, but the reasoning is tendentious. To begin with, it privileges the physical threat from non-state groups, which has always existed, above more pervasive causes of death and injury. In the last decade, atrocities by non-state actors have killed and terrorised some thousands of people worldwide; war waged ostensibly to prevent them has killed and terrorised hundreds of thousands. The slow-motion calamity of climate change is the greatest risk to ecology and society that the world has ever faced, but is buried near the end of Britain's list of security worries, as is another global human security crisis: endemic absolute poverty.[212] A heavily militarised world, as a systemic cause of insecurity in its own right, is not mentioned at all.

In addition to accentuating the threat from non-state groups, the strategy's militarised response to this misrepresents the nature of the problem. There is little that high military spending, an influx of teenage infantrymen, or new attack submarines can do to reduce the risk from small insurgent groups acting in the midst of Western societies. The heavily militarised 'war on terror' has probably made us all less safe, not more. Britain's involvement in the Iraq and Afghanistan wars seem to have figured among the main motives behind the London bombings of 2005 and the murder of Lee Rigby in Woolwich in 2013, for example.[213] The war in Afghanistan certainly disrupted al-Qa'ida groups, but only as fish are when a stick is jabbed into a pond. Meanwhile, Islamist militants have leveraged widespread discontent with America's incoherent 'war on terror' and Britain's share in it to swell their numbers and spread their doctrine. Their main stumbling block has not been Western military might, but the humane resilience of the majority of Muslims to the violent dogmas of extremism.

In certain respects, Britain's social culture is our best answer to the prospect of violent extremism. It helps that our society is becoming more multicultural, with a generally strong balance between discrete and integrated cultural identities, which is vital for sustainable social diversity. The principle of rights for all people of all communities is enshrined in legislation such as the Human Rights Act and the Equality Act, supported by an established tradition of welfare provision when necessary to help secure those rights. That this is now being eroded has consequences for the country's security. Economic inequality is on the rise, which is marginalising minority communities; welfare is being rolled back, inflaming disaffection. Britain joined the US on what George W Bush notoriously dubbed a 'crusade' in Muslim countries; the Latin root of that word, *cruciare*, means to exorcise evil from a place by marking it with the sign of the cross.[214] By puffing up the risk of an atrocity and presenting a militarised foreign policy as the main solution, the government, following the US lead, has aggravated the alienation felt by many minority communities.

This has also distracted from the unchecked march of genuinely severe and much more urgent dangers – climate change, poverty, and the depletion of natural resources, combined with militarism, whose ideology marginalises a consensus-building approach to global problems. These systemic threats to peace directly and indirectly jeopardise the security of every person on earth. They have no military solutions because they are first and foremost matters of justice. Their primary structural causes lie in an iniquitous global economic system, dominated as it is by Western governments and corporations, which are able to exploit a deficit of genuinely inclusive and thoughtful democracy at all levels of global society. These inequitable power relations belong, among other factors, to any critical appreciation of the risk from non-state groups wishing harm on the citizens of Western countries today.

In sum, the risk of an atrocity is real but poorly explains Britain's military excess. For a better appreciation of our warrior-nation outlook, we need to interrogate our state's professed 'global responsibilities and global ambitions'. Why does one state in a world of around 200 describe its own role so grandly? Mindful, perhaps, that Britain once ruled an empire, our identity as a global leader appears to have become a necessary condition of our national sense of worth; without it, we suffer a creeping fear of failure. A post-imperial identity crisis appears to seep into our disappointment when we do not come at least close to the World Cup final or to winning almost the most medals at the Olympics. On the world stage we want a starring role, not like Belgium or Norway quietly minding our own business; we used to run the world, we are Great Britain – the clue is in the name. We are not so foolish as to imagine ourselves to be imperial masters now but, like an ageing boxer, we need to believe we still pack a punch.

The *Telegraph*, favoured media organ of the establishment, frequently runs stories bemoaning our supposedly pruned-back military might as a cause of national emasculation. The paper's editorial has warned that Britain's 'weakness reduces our global power and leaves us impotent when it comes to challenges from abroad'.[215] Remove 'global' and 'from abroad' and this reads like a man craving his Viagra, and there may be more than a little misty-eyed remembrance of imperial potency in the newspaper's lament.

There are other reasons that the British state is attached, albeit impossibly, to remaining a major military power. Some, following Tony Blair's position, value the option of military interventions abroad as a necessary, humanitarian expedient to saving lives, but under law this is a matter for collective, international decision through the United Nations. Others worry that a militarily stunted Britain would no longer be welcome at the top table of world politics, and here they do have a point.

Not all states can rub shoulders with the giants of geopolitics. If you have money, if people have to listen to you, and if you can force your will when you want to, you are in. If your political, economic and military might is waning, then you are on your way out. It is a system – or just a cabal, really – of global political organisation that privileges the powerful absolutely. Thanks to the dubious economic virtues of Oxford Street, credit cards, the housing bubble and the City's trade in other people's money, Britain remains a major world economy, but the new players are slowly edging us into the relegation zone. For now, averting our gaze from the horizon before us, we eke out an ever-fugitive, post-imperial dream of global might. This cannot last. In any case, the governments of nation states hold a steadily diminishing share of global power. The most consequential decisions affecting swathes of the world's population are not made in UN meetings or even at G20 summits, but informally on exclusive golf courses by corporate CEOs and billionaire investors. Governments are afraid of these *de facto* oligarchs and their power, so dare not upset them – by taxing them properly, for example.

Instead of moving on from our imperial past, Britain has long since hitched its wagon to America's imperial present. The government has wanted us to believe that British forces were in Iraq and Afghanistan to make us more secure, liberate the oppressed, or protect human rights (the rationale for the wars shifted as they unfolded). Whatever we make of these justifications, the main reason Britain became involved is that the US wanted it. The US selected the wars, Britain supported them and, thanks to the self-confessed missionary zeal of Tony Blair, did so with gusto. Had Britain not agreed to dispatch the troops, the US would have used its own; after all, America spends almost as much on the military as does the rest of the world combined. What the President needed most from Tony Blair was Britain's political support, in order to create the impression that the wars were not entirely of American provenance. This our Prime Minister was happy to provide. He even pledged more to come, promising Congress in 2003: 'Our job is to be there with you. You're not going to be alone. We will be with you in this fight for liberty.'[216]

This is true to form. Britain's special relationship with the United States has never been as special to them as to us, which leaves our government forever having to prove its worth. Britain has 'to hold up our position *vis-à-vis* the Americans', as Clement Attlee put it when justifying his post-war decision to build British nuclear warheads.[217] If the US wants an airbase on a British island in the Indian Ocean, then the people who live there are evicted; their successful legal action for the right of return is then overruled. If the US wants MI5 or the SAS to help kidnap suspected insurgents and render them to US sites for torture, it happens. The US does not want Britain to scrap Trident, partly because this would expose America's massive nuclear stockpile to judgement, so British taxpayers pour in the billions to keep the white elephant plodding extravagantly along. And if the US is playing global vigilante and wants Britain to come in on its war, British soldiers will be sent far from home and some flattering remarks will be made about the statesmanlike qualities of our Prime Minister.

Britain's defence posture candidly names the US as its primary partner in security[218] – not the European Union, United Nations, or other European governments, but a hegemonic state that has shown itself hostile to multinational approaches to global problems. While UKIP castigates the overbearing technocracy of Brussels, our country is far more beholden to Washington, with consequences that are little scrutinised in Westminster or by the media. The commentator Matthew Parris suggested that in rushing British forces to an unwinnable war in Helmand, Tony Blair was 'impatient with geography, his mind was focused on destiny'.[219] So he seems to have been, but he was not alone; Parliament, the press, and armed forces' chiefs all wanted Britain to do America's bidding in Iraq and Afghanistan. Only the public have shown consistent opposition – in opinion and to some degree in action – to Britain's first ill-judged wars of the 21st century.

Sooner or later we will have to find a new way of being a nation in the world, freed from the bankrupt belief that a worthy nation is a powerful one and a powerful nation, worthy. The role of the progressively humanitarian state pursuing shared global action by collective decision among peers is always open to us, at least in theory. For the time being, Britain is second only to the US in the industrialised world in valorising war as a means to achieve its political goals. Whether or not we think that military action was justified in the Falkland Islands, Iraq, the former Yugoslavia, Afghanistan and Iraq again, they have all been wars of choice, with potentially-viable, less-bellicose options rejected in each case.

On this record, Britain has more wars to come. Unless the country is attacked by another state, our future conflicts will not be recognisably defensive in nature. On the contrary, they will project military power with the aim of shaping the world in the interests of London and Washington, just as the government's strategic posture document indicates. Britain and the US will be wary of repeating the debacle of the Afghanistan and Iraq invasions, but both states have since sponsored the counterproductive intervention in Libya and the thus-far-aborted attempt to militarily manage the Syrian conflict. Although genuine humanitarian concerns for the ordinary people embroiled in these upheavals are part of the motive for intervention, more potent is the desire to mould the 'strategic environment', as policy wonks call it. This is why some despots get toppled, others get a handshake, and some get both, as did Saddam Hussein, the Afghan Taliban and Osama bin Laden. Like the West's wars today, those of tomorrow will be extremely expensive investments in control, bearing little relation to the physical protection of populations in the war zone or back home.

Even as US global hegemony gradually weakens, it is extending its infrastructure of global dominance, with Britain running as fast as it can to keep up. America's slippery special forces now operate in 75 countries on an annual budget of $8 billion;[220] their British counterparts are now being beefed up, too. America's gigantic spy machine, as revealed by Edward Snowden, is harvesting as much personal information on civilians worldwide as it can, so Britain's GCHQ is going for the same. The US can now dominate the skies of far-away lands by remote control and so the UK, too, is busy buying its own drone fleet, lest we get left behind. The US-UK war in Iraq is officially over, despite the violence worsening and the insurgency growing, but the US is still there. Its embassy in Baghdad – the largest in the world at over 100 acres – will now press on in the manner of H G Wells' imperial floor game to 'alter things, and build and rearrange', exerting shades of control over the region's people for as long as it can.

* * *

Militarism's dynamic of control works not only on the world, but also through the people who enact its violence. In the Falklands War, most land warfare took place at night in a series of chaotic, close-quarters infantry battles between well-trained British forces and Argentinian conscripts, who had had plenty of time to dig in defences. The veteran Vince Bramley described it as 'combat at very close quarters, hand to hand, eye to eye, very bloody stuff'.[221] Soldiers on both sides were seeing their comrades scream and collapse next to them, or get blown into pieces by mortar shells, grenades and landmines; many veterans still live with post-traumatic stress three decades on. When one such British veteran was asked whether any single aspect of his experience stood out as a main cause of his traumatic stress, he responded without hesitation: 'You've got no control.'[222]

Armed forces personnel are controlled from the moment they turn up for training, which steadily turns young civilians into operationally effective combatants by inculcating conformity with and obedience to the martial system. Whilst training includes conventional teaching of skills such as fieldcraft and handling weapons, its main objective is to reinvent how recruits think and behave.[223] Training 'breaks you down and then rebuilds you in a different way', as one veteran has put it.[224] Another described training as operating on two fronts. First, it shapes minds by 'indoctrinating' recruits into the ideological values of the military system; and second, it 'conditions' behaviours by rewarding obedience and punishing dissent, to the point where all orders are obeyed without question or pause.[225]

In 1986, the sociologist and former soldier John Hockey wrote a detailed description of military training, which in large part still stands today.[226] The training regime aims to dispossess recruits of their civilian role and build a new self-image in its place, explains

Hockey. The process operates by making absolute demands of recruits which erode self-determination, autonomy of movement, privacy and choice of personal appearance. Required to look and behave the same, recruits are anonymised and controlled. The consequence of relentless activity is fatigue; of the demands of authoritarian power, anxiety; and of the absence of civilian norms and social support, disorientation.[227] Hockey says that this 'socialisation under pressure' will 'soften' recruits in readiness for the imposition of new personal self-images, values, and definitions of personal achievement.[228]

An effect of these adversities is the deepening of peer bonds, which veterans frequently cite as the most valued benefit of an armed forces career. The growing camaraderie, for those who are not excluded from it by bullying, serves as a source of psychological freedom within a coercive system and a form of solidarity in the face of the arduous demands made by authority figures. On the other hand, it also serves the purposes of the military system. If one person fails in a task, the whole group is punished, ensuring that recruits exert peer pressure to reinforce collective compliance.[229]

Once the enculturation of values and behaviours has succeeded in gaining the willing compliance of trainees, the socialisation process enters a new, less-rigorous phase, Hockey observed. As a measure of permissiveness returns, trust and humour between commander and commanded partially offset the strictures of the training regime. Trainees might no longer respond to their superiors' gestures of leniency with relief, but rather with gratitude. With control secured through compliance rather than enforcement, the authoritarian application of power becomes less immediately necessary, although it remains omnipresent as the guarantor of military culture.

Trainers and trainees affirm hyper-masculine norms: aggression, stoicism and aversion to weakness. 'Role effectiveness' is associated with 'masculine potency', according to Hockey.[230] In the military group, the uniformity of this identity is enforced through the training process and reinforced by formal and informal (including illicit) hyper-masculine bonding rituals. Social and institutional pressures to conform create a strong insider-outsider dynamic, in which 'military' is understood in opposition to 'civilian', strength and weakness become gendered polar opposites, and values antithetical to a hyper-masculine ideal are resisted as threatening. Indeed, Hockey and others have found that weakness and failure are frequently associated with femininity or homosexuality.[231]

In sum, recruits are controlled and partly dehumanised by the system they serve in order to prepare them for war. Yet despite the tough training and conditioning of the military regime, and in some respects because of it, exposure to the traumas of warfare still assaults the psyche. Those most affected are infantry soldiers in prolonged or repeated front-line fighting. In the heat of warfare, soldiers cannot give voice to their strain and so help to ease it. The psyche 'buries' it, only to let it resurface with typically debilitating effects at homecoming or on discharge from the forces. Traumatically stressed personnel tend to turn to alcohol to help manage the effects, which can make matters worse. Compared with the general population, drinking habits deemed harmful to health are three times as common among troops deployed to Iraq or Afghanistan.[232] The heaviest drinkers are the youngest personnel deployed in front-line roles.[233]

Unsurprisingly, being shot at is among the most stressful experiences for a soldier, but still greater strain ensues from killing other people at close quarters or seeing others killed.[234] With few exceptions, the act of killing assaults the psyche of those who do it or witness it, but soldiers in war have no control over their situation – no freedom to choose whether to continue or stop. It is actually illegal to stop and leave; the crime is desertion, which since 2006 has carried a maximum sentence of life imprisonment.[235]

Many of the mental health conditions that soldiers experience reflect the conscientious, desperate rebellion of their own humanity against the base dehumanisaton of war. We think of these as 'mental health problems' – and they are – but the primary injury is to the soul. The psychiatrist Peter Marin was among the first to propose that conscience played a role in the stress reactions of soldiers, which he characterised as their 'moral pain'.[236] Whilst such reactions are commonly stigmatised as part of a mental health 'disorder', the experience, while highly stressful, can also be understood as the healthy response of a morally functional individual. A British Iraq War veteran told me that, given his war experiences, he would have thought that something was wrong with himself if he had not been feeling a stress reaction afterwards.[237]

Some of the moral and pastoral challenges of warfare fall to the padre – the military chaplain – but these too are tightly controlled by the system they work in. According to Nicholas Mercer, a former senior army officer who has since joined the Anglican priesthood, chaplains who speak out about abuses or challenge the chain of command are often made to be quiet. He was speaking from experience. When he tried to stop abuses of Iraqi detainees by British forces at the Umm Qasr interrogation centre – later detailed in a report by the International Committee of the Red Cross – he said he 'was silenced by the Ministry of Defence'.[238] By his own account, he was 'forced to run the gauntlet of some fairly unpleasant behaviour', which he noted would be an intimidating experience for a young chaplain at the beginning of his or her career.[239] In a letter to *The Tablet*, he wrote that he had known chaplains and other officers who had been sacked for doing their job.[240]

Perhaps the most complete example of the controlled consciousness of the agent of warfare is that of the drone operator, who remotely pilots an aircraft on the other side of the world. Operators of American drones work in pairs, sitting together in a small, dark room in Nevada, staring into a bank of screens for shifts of up to 10 hours at a time. The drone gets its name from its sound, like that of a bee, but the operators hear nothing but the whirr of their computers' cooling fans; the job is mostly watching, waiting and being bored. For days or weeks, they spy on their monochrome, pixelated enemies from the disembodied, infra-red eyes of their drone as it circles high in the sky, thousands of miles away. Often, the operators get to know the daily routines of their targets – when they get up, where they go, where their families live – until the kill order comes through.

Manipulating hand-held controllers like those used for videogames, one operator flies the drone in while the other guides a Hellfire missile to a final, soundless flash of light that blanks the screen with white. When it clears, only scattered blotches of white are left on the screen; these are the bits of bodies glowing hot in the aircraft's infra-red camera. The operators will not know whom they were watching or why they had to kill them, or who else might have been in the house they destroyed. They will not even have known the person giving the kill order, nor the constant observer who watched their every action on another screen from another remote location who knows where.[241]

Given the remoteness of their location in relation to their warfare, drone operators can come surprisingly close as witnesses to its inhumane effects, but in all other respects they are in the dark. Orders are made somewhere else and people are killed somewhere else; their stuffy room of screens is the one place where nothing happens. They are dehumanised not only by the killing that is the substance of their job, but also by their ignorance of its purposes and near-total lack of autonomy in respect of it. Their paralysis as human beings – which is to say, sensing, thinking, choosing, loving beings – is almost absolute, save for the option of walking out. A moment ago I described them as agents of warfare, but this is true in only the thinnest sense, for these human operators are almost wholly reduced to an inanimate part of the war machine, as remotely controlled as the drones they remotely control. Even so, they have to witness and verify their own kills, peering into their grainy grey screens to check that the person they were supposed to eviscerate is indeed in bits.

Brandon Bryant, who flew drones for several years, described to *GQ* magazine one scene he watched on the heat-revealing infra-red screen after his kill:

> 'The smoke clears, and there's pieces of the two guys around the crater. And there's this guy over here, and he's missing his right leg above his knee. He's holding it, and he's rolling around, and the blood is squirting out of his leg, and it's hitting the ground, and it's hot. His blood is hot. But when it hits the ground, it starts to cool off;

the pool cools fast. It took him a long time to die. I just
watched him. I watched him become the same colour as
the ground he was lying on.'[242]

When they eventually leave the US air force, drone operators are
awarded a scorecard showing their total number of kills. Brandon
Bryant's read: 'Total enemies KIA: 1,626.'[243] War by remote control
is truly, coldly remote, but the killing is still killing: 'blood is hot'.

Now Britain has its own small but growing drone fleet operated
from Waddington in Lincolnshire. The same base is also home to
the annual RAF show, where families can watch military planes fly
past for £62 (£118 if you want to sit down).[244] For a premium,
families can buy a VIP experience in enclosures named after Hugh
Trenchard and 'Bomber' Harris, architects of the Second World War
massacres of the residential areas of German cities, in which 800,000
people were killed.[245] In that war, the vain expectation of the bomber
offensive had been that the mass-murder of civilians would create
such a 'moral effect' in German society that Hitler would
surrender.[246] By naming the spectator areas after these RAF
luminaries, the air show implicitly celebrates as heroic their policy
of massacre. From these vantage points, surrounded by the arms
trade logos of Boeing, BAE, Raytheon and others, mum, dad and
the kids can watch a Lancaster fly over. Perhaps this year they will
get a peek at its successor, the Reaper drone, while waving the Union
Flag 'as befits children of an imperial people'.

* * *

For all its ambitions of holding on to Britain's warrior-nation
status, our government worries that this vision bores the body
politic. It does. The public generally has a high opinion of soldiers
and likes the idea of Britain as an important state, but this interest
is generally casual, not passionate, and does not translate
straightforwardly into committed support for war. Nor does it
necessarily endorse the national power-posturing of the government's
security strategy. So, in 2007, with armed forces recruitment in

decline and polls showing public opposition to its wars, the government commissioned a report 'to identify ways of encouraging greater understanding and appreciation of the armed forces by the British public'.[247] The implication was that we, the public, were letting the side down. Equally evidently, the government had a particular 'understanding' of the armed forces in mind. For sure, they were not hoping for keener public awareness of why and how war attacks the minds and bodies of those who enact it. They wanted us to appreciate the troops' courage, not their suffering and doubts, and thus enrol our support for 'the work that they do in our name',[248] especially the government's wars in Iraq and Afghanistan. The study was ostensibly aimed at improving the social standing of the people of the armed forces, but it was really the state's project for the state's purposes; most of the people it consulted were senior establishment figures rather than personnel in the ranks.[249] The tacit hope appears to have been that if the public did more to cheer on the armed forces, we would also cheer on the state's wars.

The study's report, *National Recognition of our Armed Forces*, made 40 recommendations: more public military events, more cadet forces in state schools, more outreach programmes, and links with sporting organisations. Such promotional initiatives can build public support for the men and women of the armed forces, but not critical appreciation of their experiences or the wars they fight in. In other words, they are ideal PR but poor education, and so as likely to undermine public understanding as to enhance it. Nevertheless, most of the recommendations were implemented and the ploy almost worked. Public support for the armed forces, which was already high, stayed that way, and the state made inroads into civilian culture with militarist values, particularly by targeting the young through the education system. But the government was still unable to convert this into support for its wars. In 2010, two years after the report, Armed Forces Minister Bill Rammell betrayed his frustration by effectively warning the public not to lose their stomach for war.[250] Perhaps we are the squeamish lot he thinks we are, but the sterilised spectacle of Armed Forces Day is not going to redeem us on that score. Perhaps, on the other hand, the public recognised the wars in Iraq and Afghanistan for the impetuous American adventures they were.

The report's cornucopia of initiatives reveals the failure of successive governments since 9/11 to convince the public that the UK's share of distant wars is a necessary guarantor of either security or human rights. The British state and its establishment allies believe it needs to be able to fight future wars; it worries about whether it will be able to do so without the body politic on board; and it is urgently working to ensure that the public are prepared to support the political decisions required. Since the government has been unable to swing the public behind its wars, it is going for the next best thing: the normalisation of militarist values and worldviews by embedding them in society. The state's 'ambition' to 'shape the global environment' undoubtedly includes moulding the public's prevailing attitude into one of support for future wars, or at least polite indifference. The means employed to achieve this – the initiatives in the *National Recognition* report among them – aim to distance the public from the reality of war as horrific, while generating a romanticised public conception of war as heroic. As such, the home-front battle for hearts and minds is just as much a project of control as the world-shaping scheme it is supposed to serve.

We ought to be concerned. It might have failed to win our support for its recent wars, but the government's power to elicit public compliance and shape social culture through the education system, the media, and legislation is prodigious. So is its chutzpah in ignoring public opinion when it wants to, as it did after the huge march against the Iraq war in 2003. The political theorist Margaret Canovan writes:

> 'By historical standards, these states [modern liberal democracies] represent astonishing concentrations of collective power, wielding a degree of control over their territory and receiving a level of co-operation from their citizens that earlier despots would have envied ... Even more remarkably, these states use relatively little raw

coercion: far more of their power is a matter of mobilising consensus and directing compliance.'[251]

To this end, the state marshals and manipulates cultural symbols that tap into our needs, desires and hopes. When the Queen is sailed down the Thames for her Jubilee, she is a passive, controlled person; her behaviour is as determined by others as that of the security guard who stands stock-still next to her. But she is active as a symbol, mobilised on behalf of the state. The Union flags that line the riverbanks are not just waved in the air, they are waved at the Queen, confirming the public's loyalty as devotees of the state she represents. The national flag is an example of an *empty signifier*: a symbol whose meaning is not fixed but rather filled with whatever significance is conferred to it by those who use or witness it.[252] Even so, the flag's meaning is constant in one respect: it affirms the state as guardian of the people. Whether the vision it symbolises is one of aggressive nationalism or just a shared sense of social belonging, the Union flag always indicates the state as that vision's guarantor. It is therefore mobilised, as is the public fêting of soldiers on Armed Forces Day, as a means to generate a consensus of compliance among the public.

Propaganda trades on empty signifiers all the time and the military sphere has oodles of them: the remembrance poppy, Remembrance Day, and the name Help for Heroes are among many examples. Even the armed forces themselves are their own cultural symbol – as our heroes. Now this toolbox of indeterminate symbols has a new joiner – the Military Covenant – a presupposed, mutual commitment between the state, the public, and the armed forces. The armed forces sacrifice themselves for the nation, so the argument for the Covenant goes, therefore 'the whole nation has a moral obligation to [them] and their families'.[253] The existence of a covenantal relationship between the nation and the armed forces is a claim, not a self-evident fact, but even as rhetoric it is fast becoming the rubric under which the government attempts to justify a militarist outlook to the public.[254]

The term 'Military Covenant' appears never to have been used in print until it appeared in an internal army document in 2000,[255]

but historic roots have been claimed for it.[256] Some sources suggest
that a military-civilian covenantal understanding stretches back to
Elizabeth I, who levied a tax in favour of injured veterans,[257] but
this appeal to history cuts both ways. If there has been a covenantal
relationship between the state and its military personnel in Britain's
past, it has been habitually weak or worse, repeatedly privileging
the state over the soldier. Queen Elizabeth might well have gestured
in good will to meet the care needs of her injured officers, but her
reign also saw navy press gangs forcing civilian sailors to man the
galleons on pain of execution. In the First World War, soldiers'
chronic shell-shock caused by relentless traumatic experiences was
put down to their moral weakness;[258] hundreds of the psychiatrically
injured were shot for cowardice.[259] When troops returned from the
Falklands in 1982, the battle-wounded were barred from London's
victory parade for 'security' reasons;[260] after an outcry in the *Mirror*,
the Ministry of Defence allowed six hand-picked, wheelchair-bound
veterans to watch the parade go by.[261] The Lord Mayor still refused
to allow blinded veterans to join the procession: 'What will they
see?' he asked.[262] As these examples suggest, the state's historical
attitude to veterans has often been appalling. Even today, despite
the Military Covenant rhetoric, the government leans heavily on
charities – the Big Society – to fulfil its duty of care to veterans who
are homeless or housing-insecure, have drug or alcohol
dependencies, are unemployed, or require long-term support.

Notwithstanding the shaky historical claims for the Military
Covenant, it does have the potential to coax the government into
meeting its duty of care for veterans more effectively. With a watered-
down version of the Covenant now enshrined in the 2011 Armed
Forces Act, charities like the Army Families Federation are already
using it to hold Ministers to account. Be that as it may, its primary
purpose lies elsewhere: as a bugle call for public support of the
armed forces at war. General Richard Dannatt's tones of hyperbole
made this clear in 2007 when he was head of the army:

> 'I have become increasingly concerned about the
> growing gulf between the Army and the Nation. I am

not talking about the support that we get from Her
Majesty's Government and to a large extent I am not
talking about public finances. Rather, I am talking about
how the Nation as a whole views the Army... [T]he real
covenant is with the population at large – the Nation.
The covenant says that we do what we do in your name;
soldiers do not ask why; but they do ask for respect and
honour for doing what they have been sent to do with
courage and professionalism...'[263]

This claim hinges on several sleights of rhetoric. The soldier's
enlistment contract is with the state, not the 'population at large'.
The army's public service ought to be measured by how effectively
it serves the public interest, rather than merely how well it fights
whatever war the state chooses for it; only a naïf would presume
that what the state wants and what the country needs must be the
same thing. Whilst it is often said that the troops 'put themselves
at risk to keep us safe', as the Queen intones every Christmas,[264] it
is the state that puts them at risk and this does not necessarily keep
us safe. The invasions of Iraq and Afghanistan have probably had
the opposite effect. Given the horrors of warfare that many troops
experience first-hand, we ought to empathise and show solidarity
with their position in relation to their employer, but gratitude is
another matter. Why should we thank the troops for fighting distant
wars which the public oppose and which seem to put the country
at risk? Rather than fulfilling its duty of care to its soldiers, the
government is using them to manufacture public support for its
wars, while spinning its specious claim that we are 'morally obliged'
to be grateful.

The Military Covenant rubric in its various forms now frames most
of the support-our-troops initiatives launched by the *National
Recognition* report. A so-called Community Covenant, to which most
local authorities are now committed, releases funds for local projects
with a military theme. The scheme paid £130,000 for an RAF-themed
children's adventure playground in Carterton, Oxfordshire, for
example.[265] A Corporate Covenant commits businesses to giving

veterans a fair crack at getting work – a right they have in law anyway – and to support initiatives like Armed Forces Day.

Funded by fines levied from the banks' LIBOR fraud of 2012, the Covenant has sent the armed forces' PR machine into overdrive and sprouted hundreds of new local events and national schemes. Among these are homecoming parades in town centres; away-days at military bases for businesses; ostentatiously militarised security for mega-events like the Olympics; and pre-kick-off medal award ceremonies on Premier League match days. In the spirit of the *National Recognition* report, armed forces recruiters and military marketing have become far more pervasive in civilian life: in schools, job centres, community buildings, leisure centres, at cultural events, and throughout the annual Remembrance Festival. They are also piggy-backing on the First World War commemorations with events that present the war as heroic derring-do.[266]

The central propaganda vehicle under the Military Covenant is now the annual Armed Forces Day. Launched in 2009 after the *National Recognition* report recommended it, the event's scale now rivals the British Legion's Remembrance Festival in November. It is a nationwide, soft recruitment jamboree, described as a 'thrilling spectacle with a plethora of explosions'.[267] After its lacklustre beginnings, the day is now backed by extensive TV advertising with the tagline 'Show Your Support' and events are planned in over 100 towns annually. In order to boost the event's mass appeal, the armed forces have asked celebrities to draft endorsements, which tend to have a generic flavour, like this one by the Archbishop of York, John Sentamu: 'I hope as many of you as possible take this opportunity to show your support for our brave servicemen and servicewomen all around the world as they put their lives at risk on a daily basis to protect our freedoms and the freedoms of many. They are all real heroes...'[268]

By lionising and in some cases fetishising the armed forces, initiatives like Armed Forces Day serve to normalise a swollen military force as part of the healthy order of society – even one facing no military threats for the foreseeable future. As in war, so in the propaganda battle at home, the state controls the soldiers as a body, making them stand and march as an heroic emblem of nationhood. The stage-managed fêting of soldiers reduces them once again to means, rather than ends; in making a collective cultural icon of them, it submerges them as individual persons. In these set-pieces, as the Falklands veteran Gus Hales has said, we the public are rarely allowed to hear soldiers' own voices, which may be complex and, from the state's point of view, intolerably unpredictable.

* * *

The social group that the military PR machine most needs to charm is children and young people, particularly those in the poorest neighbourhoods. As head of army recruitment, Colonel (now Brigadier) David Allfrey explained to the *New Statesman*, the process of recruiting the teenage soldier begins at the age of seven, when his family takes him to an air show and he leaves wanting to be a parachutist. 'From then the army is trying to build interest by drip, drip, drip,' Allfrey said, until recruiters, whom he described as 'skilled salesmen', visit the child's school.[269] In that span of around eight years, the same child will have encountered cadets, military parades, recruiters in the streets, Armed Forces Day, the romanticisation of war at the cinema and on the Xbox, and any number of other instances of drip, drip, drip. If the child does not sign up, the army hopes that he or she will at least cheer them on when called to do so.

The Ministry of Defence is perplexingly emphatic that the armed forces 'never visit schools for recruitment purposes'[270] and that cadet forces have nothing to do with recruiting,[271] but its own documents and occasional slips of the tongue prove otherwise. In 2005, its youth strategy described schools visits as a 'powerful tool for facilitating recruitment especially if the skills developed through curricular activities have a direct bearing on military requirements'.[272] In 2008, the Ministry told the Defence Committee that 'recruiting teams… visit schools' and that army visits 'enable recruiters to access the school environments'.[273] In 2011, it admitted that recruitment and awareness are 'the two principal benefits to Defence' of its youth engagement work.[274] It has taken longer to admit that the recruitment value of cadet forces now inspires their expansion in state schools, but a Ministry source has been quoted as saying exactly that.[275] So, what young people already knew to be true is true – recruitment *is* one of the main purposes of the forces' youth engagement through schools and the cadets.

Increasingly anxious to fill the ranks, especially the perennially undermanned infantry, the army openly targets so-called 'pre-eligibles': children not yet of recruitment age. Its online recruitment programme for 14–16 year olds, called *Camouflage*, celebrates 'awesome armour', 'big guns', and 'wonder weapons', linking through to the jobs site.[276] For the youngest children, the armed forces partner with the wealthy welfare charity SSAFA to produce Camo Day, an event for primary school children linked to Armed Forces Day. Five and six year olds dressed as soldiers in camouflage paint march up and down, salute, hang out with real soldiers, and chant the fundraising slogan: 'Dress up, blend in, put your pennies in the tin.'[277] In 2014, Camo Day's militarist play was offered as a way for schools to commemorate the start of the First World War. In view of the charity's support for psychiatrically and physically injured personnel, it is striking that its staff did not think better of an event that gives primary school children the impression that war is fun.

The demographic of armed forces recruitment is heavily skewed by age, gender, ethnicity and particularly social class. Commissioned officers are drawn mostly from upper-middle class families up to and including royalty. Enlisted personnel, whose highest rank is one rung below the lowest commissioned officer rank, tend to be recruited from working class neighbourhoods, with the most disadvantaged providing the main recruiting ground for non-technical roles in the army. Very few middle class teenagers enlist in the army, which is rarely a job of choice for people with means and opportunity. Whilst some young people from poor backgrounds join up because it has long been a first-choice career in their military family, others escape to the army as their only apparent, economically-viable option.

The army's recruitment efforts are concentrated in economically depressed regions: central Scotland, north-east and northwest England, Wales, and the West Country. In Scotland, for example, the armed forces visited approximately four-fifths of state schools in the two years from September 2010.[278] Within disadvantaged regions, schools with the most deprived catchment areas are visited most often, where civilian jobs are fewest and more children struggle academically. Arbroath Academy, the most frequently contacted school in Scotland, with some 31 armed forces visits in two years,[279] is one of the country's poorest: 29% of its students take free school meals.[280]

Having segmented their target group carefully, recruiters provide literature that comes nowhere close to describing a military career fairly.[281] The opening page of the infantry jobs guide professes to be 'telling it like it is', but nowhere in the brochure's 12 pages will its readers find the word 'kill'.[282] Nor does it mention the restrictive contractual obligations that enlistment involves: if trainees do not choose to leave during the first few months, they are prevented from leaving for four years or more and will be incarcerated if they try. If the literature wanted to ensure a 16 year old had all the facts before deciding whether to enlist, it would not omit such critical information, but then readers would surely wonder why such glamorous, exciting jobs require the law to prevent people from leaving them for so long. David Buck, a veteran of the Kosovo conflict, has described the materials that army recruiters gave him:

'They sit you down in the recruiting office and give you brochures and, you know, all the bumf about it. And I was just sat there reading it and thinking, "Wow! I want to do this". The sort of propaganda was really effective, you know, to a kid… They show you all the pictures of the adventure training like abseiling, skiing… Being so young I was easily manipulated… It doesn't show someone with their head blown off, does it, or whose child has just been killed – [it] doesn't show that.'[283]

The youngest recruits from the poorest backgrounds are substantially more likely than others to be given a job in the infantry,[284] which is generally the most dangerous part of the armed forces. In Afghanistan, the risk of injury and fatality among infantrymen has been seven times that in the rest of the armed forces, for example,[285] and the rate of trauma-related mental health problems in the infantry has been about twice that found in the army's support roles.[286] Unlike the training offer in the navy and RAF, and for certain technical army trades, infantry recruits get little that they can transfer to a civilian job when they leave, usually after about 10 years. In tending to enlist youngest, straight from school, these recruits also miss out on civilian education and training opportunities for 16–18 year olds, which are generally superior to those on offer in the army.[287] The army presents the infantry as an opportunity to enhance the social mobility of young people from poor backgrounds, but recruiting from age 16 could also be said to exploit people in a weak socio-economic position as they go through the most impressionable stage of their development. The poor training offer, the restrictive legal obligations of enlistment, and the sanitised, glamorised picture of military life presented in recruitment literature, all count against the narrative of opportunity that recruiters present.

Despite recruiters' state-of-the-art marketing and the razzmatazz of their salesmanship, they often face a culture of scepticism among teachers, parents and young people themselves; fewer 16 and 17 year olds are enlisting. The government has reacted by shifting focus. Rather than merely trying to persuade sceptical young people to enlist, the state is conditioning their cultural environment to be more accepting of militarist values and worldviews. It is as if the government has taken a line from its security strategy – 'applying all our instruments of power and influence to shape the global environment'– and translated it to the cultural milieu of young people.[288] It is a colonial project in the same spirit as the occupation of the 'comprehensively Indian' territories of H G Wells' floor game, but the islands up for grabs are the minds of children.

Cadet forces in state schools are being expanded at a cost of £11 million to 2015, as part of a drive towards establishing a cadet unit into every school that wants one.[289] Defying criticism from teaching unions, the Department for Education is allowing veterans without a degree to train as teachers in half the time usually required.[290] It is also prioritising funding for education projects run by ex-military personnel, with £8 million of grants made in the scheme's first two years.[291] The measures, which belong to the Department for Education's Military Skills and Ethos Programme, launched in 2012, amount to the partial militarisation of education.

When the Education Secretary, Michael Gove, defended the policy, he submitted that '[e]very child can benefit from the values of a military ethos',[292] but what this means is undefined beyond a vague list of uniformly positive virtues: 'self discipline, resilience, teamwork and leadership'.[293] The academic Paul Dixon advances a longer list of plausibly 'military' values, namely 'patriotism, unity, hierarchy, discipline, obedience, authoritarianism, pessimism, cynicism'. He suggests we contrast these with 'democratic values': 'equality, diversity, dissent, participation, autonomy'.[294] By this reading, a 'military ethos' prizes hierarchy over equality, unity over diversity, obedience over autonomy, discipline over dissent. Michael Gove's department has yet to explain the educational rationale for his scheme or provide evidence of any benefit, beyond two studies limited to cadet forces.[295] In privileging certain values over others, and in the absence of a clear educational rationale, the Military Ethos in Schools initiative is a muddled and ideologically-driven experiment on young people.

The government's notion of a 'military ethos' is also selective in its appreciation of armed forces culture. It overlooks the armed forces' prevalent bullying and sexual harassment, for example. It argues for 'self-discipline', but ignores that military order depends principally on something else: unquestioning obedience. It uncritically valorises the highly gendered construction of the soldier, whose role is founded on a limited set of virtues associated with hyper-masculinity – stoicism, the strength to conquer, freedom from doubt. Can it be healthy for schools to allow models of discipline rooted in a culture of patriarchy and masculine dominance to displace models that value mutuality in relationships, a listening curiosity, and reflective responsibility including dissent? As far as Michael Gove's scheme can teach positive values, good teachers are already doing it. They are able to draw out the best from their students thanks to their substantial training, which veterans being fast-tracked through the Troops to Teachers programme will not get. If ex-forces personnel train fully as teachers, instead of taking the short-cut, doubtless they can be just as good, but there is no military virtue that enables a veteran to learn the job in half the time it takes everyone else.

One reason for embedding the military and its value system into education is that the state has long looked upon the armed forces as the final guarantor of order: *In emergency, break glass, release army.* The forces can be mobilised, sometimes appropriately, sometimes not, for any unexpected urgency. They ran the Green Goddesses during the fire strikes of 1977 and 2002, made up the security guard shortfall for the Olympics in 2012, and joined the response to the flooding of 2014. The army was even on the cusp of deployment during the miners' strike of 1984 to transport coal to power stations.[296] Now, they are a magic wand to wave over what the government perceives as ill-discipline in schools.

Another reason is simply that the government wants teenagers to join the ranks of the military, or at least to shape the next generation of citizen-true-believers to glorify Britain's wars. Certainly, the Military Ethos Programme has helped some school students to achieve more,[297] but that is what happens with an injection of £8 million. The scheme's benefits should be weighed against the opportunity cost. For the social commentator Simon Barrow, a 'military ethos' is a world away from the real needs of young people:

'The skills and aptitudes young people need most in a changing, diverse and conflictual world are those that foster cooperation, creative nonviolence, conflict transformation, restorative justice, peacemaking, and a

sense of moral community that eschews rather than
glorifies violence…'[298]

Imagine how far £8 million would go in supporting young people
to deal with conflict well, with the emphasis on enhancing their
choices rather than enforcing their discipline.

* * *

In the world, in the armed forces, and in society, militarism
occupies its psychological, cultural and physical territory by methods
subtle and gross: pacifying thought, controlling bodies, and
commandeering the politics of global relations. As a dynamic of
imperial control, it meets resistance with violence, most obviously
through war but also, for example, by the punitive incarceration of
dissenting soldiers. When resistance is weak or absent, the effect of
militarism is to oppress, which is to say, after Paulo Freire, that it
domesticates public consciousness.[299]

The creeping invasiveness of militarism is pushed back every time
people within the scope of its dominance determine not to participate
in its game. First among these are young men and women who
refuse to be wielded as instruments of violence in war, described
famously by Albert Einstein as 'the pioneers of a warless world'.
Refusal to kill is as old as war itself; cases of objectors during the
Roman Empire have been recorded, for example. In the First World
War, 20,000 British men refused to be conscripted, of whom 6,000
were sent to prison and in some cases were so harshly treated that
they died there.[300] Mass refusals were seen again in the Second
World War, when 60,000 men and 1,000 women applied for
exemptions from military service.[301]

Britain abolished conscription in 1960, but among those who
now enlist voluntarily moral doubts can still develop and often do,
leading personnel in some cases to a conscientious refusal to kill.
In recent times, a tiny few of these individuals have reached the
attention of the British public. One was Vic Williams, who went
Absent Without Leave rather than deploy to the Gulf War in 1990:

'I was a keen soldier with a strong sense of duty, and that was the hardest decision I have ever had to make. But like a lot of the guys, I did not think that what we were being asked to do was justified. My conscience wouldn't let me take part in pure naked aggression.'[302]

Vic Williams was sentenced to 14 months in prison for desertion and for speaking out against the war, which is unlawful for military personnel; Amnesty regarded him as a prisoner of conscience.[303]

A number of British veterans hit the headlines for refusing to fight in the Iraq and Afghanistan wars, such as Ben Griffin, Joe Glenton, Michael Lyons and Malcolm Kendall-Smith. Unlike Vic Williams, Ben Griffin was allowed to leave the army with an honourable discharge after telling his Commanding Offer he no longer believed in the Iraq war. He was the exception. Most objectors whose stand has reached the press have been punished by incarceration, demotion, and dishonourable discharge, their conscientious motives doubted. If the intention is to cow them, it tends to fail: many such veterans now number among our wars' most eloquent and persuasive critics.

Occasional media attention on these few individuals should not be construed to mean that conscientiously informed objections are rare in the armed forces. Certainly, the number of formal registrations for discharge on grounds of conscience is usually small, but the procedure is long-winded, complicated, and not made available to personnel in writing. If personnel have heard of the term 'conscientious objection' at all, they are often unaware that it refers to any profoundly felt scruple about war; it is not reserved for Quakers and Jehovah's Witnesses facing conscription. Those who do apply can earn the ire of other personnel who feel betrayed by a 'turncoat' colleague, making the process a risky road to travel. Applicants might well see their claim dismissed, as Michael Lyons' was, which leaves the objector with no conscientious option other than 'refusing to soldier', a provocative stand that brings the military machine down on their head. Most personnel with an objection deal with it in their own way: the simplest option is to give notice and leave the forces as soon as possible, but the contractual obligations of enlistment can prevent new recruits from doing so for a period of years.[304] Other options for objectors, far from ideal, include going Absent Without Leave, as Joe Glenton did, or telling their troop leader that they have a drug problem; true or not, it leads to instant dismissal.

How many conscientious objectors – or doubters, at least – might still be riding out their military career, sandwiched between the duty of their job and that of their conscience? It is impossible to know, but the prevalence of mental health problems in the forces yields a clue. Combat stress, as well as its common consequences such as heavy drinking and violent behaviour, typically have a strong conscientious component, namely a visceral, somatic reaction against killing and being conditioned to kill.[305] There has yet to be a study to investigate whether Post-Traumatic Stress Disorder is associated with conscientious reactions to warfare, but the hypothesis is plausible. If there is such a link, then current armed forces personnel with some degree of moral objection to warfare could number in the thousands. If this seems far-fetched, consider that research by the official US historian of the Second World War, S L A Marshall, found that four out of five US infantrymen refused to fire their rifle or aimed to miss.[306] Of the infantryman whose training has insufficiently conditioned him to kill on command, Marshall said, 'At the vital point [of firing his weapon] he becomes a conscientious objector.'[307] From the First World War to the present, almost all the killing has been done by heavy artillery or aerial bombardment, from a distance that has kept personnel from the traumatically stressful experience of watching bodies tear apart under the barrage. The development of such 'stand-off' technology has massively extended the potential scale of mass violence, but strategic reliance on infantry troops remains. Their job, which includes to kill at close range, continues to bring them literally face-to-face with the inhumanity of warfare.

Besides rebellion from the ranks, others responsible for supporting the military system of control have also spoken out. Richard Pendleton, who used to write the publicity materials for army jobs, is the only former executive to have publicly criticised the ad agencies' manipulative messaging to children and young people. 'I'm really uncomfortable with… how we sold the army to young people; I feel like I was party to some fairly questionable stuff,' he admitted.[308] As an army recruiter, Martin McGing would take the SA-80 rifle into schools to get children excited about becoming soldiers. He now regrets his involvement: 'Kids loved it,' he said, but the approach was 'wrong' and 'not honest'.[309]

School teachers, parents and pupils have also taken a stand. Although the armed forces visit most schools, even some primary schools,[310] some head teachers refuse to host them. One such refusenik institution is the Trinity Catholic School in Leamington. Its Principal, Chris Gabbett, believes it is wrong to encourage children to enlist from age 16 when they are 'still choosing the appropriate pathways to enable them to be consciously, politically and socially fully involved in an adult world'.[311] He believes the minimum age for recruitment should be 18, which would bring it in line with the age of adult responsibility that applies to buying a drink, signing a contract, and even playing *Call of Duty*. Most of the rest of the world now recruits from age 18; the UK is the only state in the EU and one of only 19 worldwide that still enlist 16 year olds.[312]

Although teenagers are self-evidently more susceptible than adults to the glossy nonsense presented by recruiters, they are far from being passively uncritical as a group. Young people have been among the most articulate and determined agents of resistance, sometimes leaving their politically tamer teachers in the shade. One school student told me that she and her friends had asked recruiters so many difficult questions that the army gave up on her school for good.[313] Another, Lorna McKinnon, aged 14 from Bellahouston Academy in Glasgow, told the *Sunday Herald* in 2007:

> 'I thought school was the one place you could get away from the horror of the Iraq war, so I was shocked to go into the playground one day and see a helicopter and 20 army guys trying to recruit us. This was without my or my parents' permission, and I had no choice but to listen… but they won't get me.'[314]

Now the youth organisation The Woodcraft Folk has joined the growing campaign to raise the minimum age of recruitment to 18:

> 'We want every young person in the UK to have opportunities after education that aren't limited to the military. We believe that if any young person has no other option, they have been failed. We want every young person in the UK to be able to access positive youth work and education that tackles and solves the problems that young people face, rather than masking them with disciplinary systems.'[315]

* * *

In colonising the outlook of children, occupying the bodies of soldiers, and dominating relations between nation states, a culture of militarism diminishes us and turns our humanity to inhumane purposes. As militarism domesticates and controls, it stands against freedom: not the unbounded liberty of consumer capitalism that Western wars profess to defend at home, nor the enforced liberty that they profess to impose abroad, but the freedom of our common desire to be more fully human. One of Paulo Freire's insights was that the journey from oppression to freedom is the very thing that makes us more human; the process itself will 'return to the people what truly belongs to them', namely their 'stolen humanity', he said.[316] To my mind, veterans who felt that the military regime entrapped their conscience, and so left it and turned their skills to challenging militarism and war, testify to this process of re-humanisation. In Freire's terms, they are no longer 'beings for another'.[317] They prove the political potency of moral imagination, which they show is at work even within the domesticating structures of militarism. Their stand ought to challenge us all to look upon our own participation in the controlling dynamic of militarism that they have renounced.

The shift from war to peace begins with a kind of turning, as individuals and societies – a humane movement of the spirit. It moves away from somnambulant acquiescence in structures of violence and towards critical awareness expressed in action for change. In this movement lies the mettle of our humanity. Richard Feynman, the celebrated physicist who helped to design the atom bomb, characterised the shift he made – too late, he felt – in terms of thinking versus not thinking. He was with colleagues at Los Alamos nuclear research laboratory when news reached them that their bomb had destroyed the city of Hiroshima. He was asked later how he had responded:

'The only reaction I remember... was a very considerable elation and excitement and there was all kind of parties and people got drunk... I was involved with this happy thing and also drinking and drunk... at the same time as the people were dying and struggling in Hiroshima ...'

'[T]he original reason to start the project... was the Germans were a danger, [which] started me off on a process of action... to try to make the bomb work,... to make it a "worse" bomb... With any project like that you continue to work to try to get "success", having decided to do it. But what I did immorally, I would say, was not to remember the reason that I said I was doing it, so that when the reason changed, which was that Germany was defeated, not [a] single thought came to my mind at all about that; that that meant, now, that I [had] to reconsider why I'm continuing to do this. *I simply didn't think...*'

'I remember being in New York with my mother in a restaurant – right after, immediately after – and... I knew how big the bomb in Hiroshima was, how big an area it covered and so on, and I realised from where we were, 59th Street, if you dropped one in 34th Street, it would spread all the way out there and all these people would be killed... and that [there] wasn't only one bomb available but it was easy to continue to make them.'[318]

Unrestricted

'What good is freedom if we are afraid to follow our conscience? What good is freedom if we are not able to live with our own actions? I am confined to a prison but I feel, today more than ever, connected to all humanity.'[319]

Camilo Mejía, who wrote these words from a military jail in Oklahoma, had led US infantry soldiers in Iraq, but soon came to see the war as 'immoral and criminal, a war of aggression, a war of imperial domination'.[320] After two weeks of leave back home, he refused to return to the war zone, which earned him time inside for desertion. 'By putting my weapon down, I chose to reassert myself as a human being,' he wrote, and he begged Iraqis' forgiveness for his part in a war that brutalised civilians.[321]

Thousands of veterans, including former conscientious objectors like Camilo, now spend their time resisting war and militarism. Often vilified as cowards, often lauded as heroes, they are neither. These resisters are ordinary people who, having experienced abnormal conditions of extreme violence, choose to reclaim their humanity that their military training, regimented system, and war mission have submerged.[322]

Ben Griffin is one such British veteran, who now believes that militarism and the wars it produces are shades of illegal, irrational and immoral. Before long, most soldiers recognise at least one of these truths, he says, and have to decide whether to put up with it or get out. The war in Iraq confronted Ben with all three. His journey from career soldier to doubting soldier and then war resister resembles those of thousands of others, but like those, is unique in its particulars. Having enlisted in the army's élite Parachute Regiment, he excelled, was swiftly promoted, and distinguished himself as a skilled and reliable soldier in Northern Ireland,

Macedonia and Afghanistan. He then passed selection for his dream job in the Special Air Service, one of the world's most capable special forces units of around 200 soldiers. His first operational posting as an SAS trooper was to Iraq. Here, too, he distinguished himself, but with growing discomfort about the mission, which was terrorising civilians in their homes and failing in its strategic objectives. It was, in other words, illegal, irrational and immoral.

During his mid-tour break, Ben returned home determined to play no further part in the war. Like most soldiers in his position, he was neither aware that his response amounted to a conscientious objection nor of his right to apply for discharge on those grounds. He thought of going on the run but instead arranged to meet his Commanding Officer, telling him, 'I don't believe in the war in Iraq and I'm not going back.'[323] Unusually, and with decency, his CO respected his choice and decided to recommend an honourable discharge, allowing Ben to leave the army within a few months. During this process he was sent to see the regimental chaplain. Despite the padre's professional responsibility to support individuals with moral doubts, he was unsympathetic.

As a civilian again, Ben spoke out about the war. The Ministry of Defence responded with legal action that imposed a lifetime injunction against revealing any of his Iraq experiences, including the dubious legality of his mission and its appalling toll on civilians. Aware that many other veterans were also angry about Britain's military ventures, he co-founded a British branch of Veterans For Peace (VFP) as part of a worldwide network of veterans committed to working for a world without war. VFP UK now has 120 members, some of whom have become activists, artists, poets, writers, public speakers and campaign organisers since leaving the forces.

Artist and VFP member Steve Pratt painted the image shown on this book's cover, *View from the Drone: Northern Pakistan (23 January 2009)*, after one such aircraft had killed at least nine members of a civilian family on that date.[324] The strike was the first authorised by Barack Obama as US President. It took place three days after he had told the world in his inauguration address that 'America is a friend of each nation, and every man, woman and child who seeks a future of peace and dignity'.[325] The drone's Hellfire missile had killed two children; a third, aged 14, was left with shrapnel in his stomach, a fractured skull and only one eye, according to reports that emerged afterwards.[326] Steve explains the genesis of the painting:

'The painting was one of several being progressed in the studio, as part of my Military Conflict series (1987– ongoing). When I heard the troubling and tragic news about civilian deaths, including children, as a result of the first drone strike authorised by Barack Obama just three days after his inauguration, *View from the Drone* materialised very quickly. I combined feelings of a "desolate unknown landscape" seen from the point of view of a remote "pilot" seated behind a computer many hundreds of miles away in a secret location, with the language of search and destroy missions where "targets are identified" but where civilians and children are simply not seen or accounted for. After so much promise in Obama's inauguration address it was as if the USA slipped back to the war exploits of previous administrations.'[327]

By the beginning of 2014, President Obama had signed off on nearly 400 further drone attacks – far more than his predecessor – resulting in a known minimum of 273 civilian deaths.[328]

View from the Drone speaks to the themes of this book: the distanced, mendacious spectacle of the 'clean war', and the dirty reality it tries to hide, namely the militarist will to impose control on the world, in which ordinary people suffer the most. The painting stands as an act of artistic resistance. By presenting us with the soulless drone's view of the distant surface of the Earth, abstracted from the life living upon it, the image confronts us with unsettling questions about our own complicity in the militarism of states, and with 'playing God' in far-away lands.

The work of VFP UK falls into three categories – education, resistance, solidarity:

> Education on the true nature of war both towards the
> public and amongst ourselves. Resistance to war and
> militarism through nonviolent action. Solidarity with
> the victims of war and those working for peace.[329]

To these ends, VFP UK works with schools to educate young people about the realities of war, speaks out in the media against the cultural celebration of militarism, collects and publishes the testimonies and opinions of veterans, and organises an annual public conference. Members are involved in peace and reconciliation work in Northern Ireland, solidarity work for Guantánamo detainees and the incarcerated American military whistle-blower Chelsea Manning, and many other forms of peacebuilding and war resistance. On Remembrance Day after the main ceremony has finished in Whitehall, veterans walk with civilian supporters to the Cenotaph under a banner reading 'Never Again' to lay a wreath of white poppies for peace.

In Northern Ireland during the Troubles, British soldiers with authority to kill were issued with yellow cards printed with their rules of engagement and marked RESTRICTED. On the same yellow card, marked UNRESTRICTED, Ben now distributes the Statement of Purpose used by Veterans for Peace worldwide:

> We, having dutifully served our nation, do hereby affirm
> our greater responsibility to serve the cause of world peace.
>
> To this end we will work, with others:
>
> - Towards increasing public awareness of the costs of
>   war.
>
> - To restrain our government from intervening, overtly
>   and covertly, in the internal affairs of other nations.
>
> - To end the arms race and to reduce and eventually
>   eliminate nuclear weapons.

- To seek justice for veterans and victims of war.

- To abolish war as an instrument of national policy.

- To achieve these goals, members of Veterans for Peace pledge to use non-violent means and to maintain an organisation that is both democratic and open, with the understanding that all members are trusted to act in the best interests of the group for the larger purpose of world peace.[330]

'iRaq', subvertising poster mashing iPod ad with maltreatment of detainees by US personnel at Abu Ghraib prison (Design: Forkscrew Graphics)

Veterans for Peace walk to the Cenotaph, 2013 (Photo: Guy Smallman)

School students in London protest against military recruiters in the education system,2007 (Photo: Stop the War Coaltion)

Graphic artist and veteran Darren Cullen lampoons the glamorisation of military life with his darkly satirical 'Be The Meat' comic, 2014 (www.spellingmistakescostlives.com)

CONCLUSION

It is spring in the park. From the café tables by the lake, we are watching tiny lumps of life: seven baby coots. Huddled in their twig nest right by the shore, their yellowy punk-rocker heads poke out from under their mother. Everyone here is quietly rapt as the chicks' squeaks and twitching beaks are answered with slimy gobbets of feed.

A woman arrives and rushes through to the water's edge. 'Look!' she almost shouts, pointing at the nest. But we are looking. By way of answer, someone says, 'Aren't they cute?' 'But… no…' the woman says, facing us to make us understand, 'I saw them when they were *eggs!*'

All morning I have had the imagined carnage of wars rattling in my thoughts as I work on this text: our history of lethal violence on a massive scale, the shame of our species. Yet here we are, strangers of the same species, enthralled in these fragile, vulnerable, baby birds, each hatched from a mystery called an egg. The quietness of our gazes shows something of our tenderer humanity. These pea-brained creatures matter to us; we are glad of them and want them to be well. A share of our affection is perhaps sentimental – 'Aren't they cute?' – but this is also a minor encounter with the fragile fullness of living things and the precariousness of their perch. We may be casual gongoozlers, but we are also witnesses.

I like to think that these vulnerable bundles of life remind us gently of who and what we, their spectators, really are. We too are alive, made of soft flesh and breakable bone. Like the birds, our lives were given from the darkness of an egg and we coddle our own young in turn. Our bodies are perennially violable, and yet our worth as living beings – and as human beings – is inalienable. If this is who and what we are, then the value judgement that wars insist we make – of other people's worthiness of life or death according to their origin – comes from forgetting it. That judgement is made only when we lose ourselves, adrift from our deeper humanity, which knows for itself the radical equality that persists between us all.

So it is that we have been so ready to war with one another through history. Yes, we have an impulse to protect by force what is valuable and vulnerable, but that motive is a humble one. It would not create empires, sell arms across the world, ponder in engineering laboratories the efficiencies of slaughter, or glamorise warfare to teenagers so as to sell them a role in it. The richer expression of our common desire to protect is found in working for a world that is less violent, more concerned to make peace work than to prepare for war. For their part, the coots have their own way of seeing rivals off: a harmless pantomime of squawking and splashing. It is a farcical kind of foreign policy, yet not nearly as preposterous as the warring imperial vanities of some of our contemporary societies.

Watching life at work in its nest, I am staggered to think that British and US forces have used types of chemical weapon that attack the processes of life itself. One of the most notorious, Agent Orange, halts or otherwise interferes with the expression of genes as cells reproduce. It does not kill by kinetic blast; it just stops life from working. This insidious weapon is not currently in use, but its variants were deployed in Malaya and Vietnam to strip vegetation of its foliage. The chemical caused malformations in animal young, including human babies, and excoriated the skin of anyone contacted, leaving lesions all over the body and life-long scarring.

The British were first to cotton on to the toxin's military potential and bought large quantities from ICI – Imperial Chemical Industries – to quell the Malayan insurgency in the 1950s. The US followed, spraying millions of gallons over the forests and fields of Vietnam in secret. (Among the dispersal aircraft used were massive twin-rotor Boeing Chinook helicopters, which RAF pilots occasionally practise landing in this park.) The purpose of Agent Orange was to destroy the natural ecology by which people lived, driving farmers from land and depriving the Viet Cong of the rural economy upon which they depended. The chemical tore through the genetic fabric of the forest canopy, undergrowth and soil; the natural ecosystem is still damaged today.

Thus, having duped or drafted ordinary Americans to turn against ordinary Vietnamese, war leaders then ordered them to attack the substrate of the life upon which civilians depended. Like all their war orders, America's leadership justified the offensive use of Agent Orange as necessary, expedient and even righteous, framing it rhetorically as a service to the American people and the world. In order to dodge allegations of war crimes, they argued that British use in Malaya gave this chemical weapon an acceptable precedent for Vietnam.[331] Arthur Galston, who first discovered the active ingredient was horrified by its use against ecosystems and the people who lived by them. He rallied his peers to campaign for a moratorium on its use, eventually succeeding.

How did the politicians, generals and soldiers come to perpetrate such a crime – a terrorist one, at that? Were they beset with a sort of existential amnesia; had they forgotten who and what they really were as human beings? Nothing more strongly than war requires such a complete occlusion of our common sensibility for other life – the visceral feeling of belonging to one other and to the earth, which defines the humane human being. Some of those who support or wage war are myopic before other life – there will always be a few who enjoy war or perpetrate it with indifference. Some, like Arthur Galston, are horrified because they have not lost their way from their own humanity and they resolve to act accordingly. Others, including many soldiers, are so controlled by the system wielding them for its violence that they have, as one veteran put it to me, 'no space to feel bad' until they leave it.[332]

If the first step towards war is the negligent forgetting of our own humanity, then we need the discipline and moral imagination not to lose our way as humane human beings. A critique of militarism depends not only on understanding better the reality of war; we need reminding of what life is, too: that we belong deeply to one another, and not only by virtue of sharing the same culture or nation. Yes, we have our common tribe and that matters, but our common humanity transcends it. Against this truth, the conceits of militarism lose their purchase: that our 'other' is our enemy, our dominance is our salvation, our wars are our peace.

The advent of Agent Orange depended on us forgetting another truth, one so fundamental to life that our survival now depends on remembering it: the earth's life is its own worth and our species lives by the grace of it. If our world has a rightful order at all then it is first an ecological one, in which every being of every species belongs in relation to the whole. At our most humane we participate in the earth rather than treat it as a resource to be plundered; at our best we claim our place but also honour the gifted and contingent nature of our existence. Militarism, which works by imposing control, is the antithesis of this ecological understanding of peace, in which every being participates mutually.

There is still another remembrance that a critique of militarism requires. Every war Britain has fought was started by ruling élites, whether our own or those of other countries. These élites have pitched ordinary people here against ordinary people over there; the generals were generally not at the front; the politicians were politically a world away. Resistance to wars has come principally from people's movements. Indeed, most of the freedoms, rights, and joys of being a society are hard-won through the struggles of people with no extraordinary political power.

This park happens to be Victoria Park in East London, frequented nowadays by well-to-do bohemians and bankers, some of whom pay for 'military fitness' sessions here, or use their iPhones to film the occasional, deafening Chinook landing practice, or indeed watch these baby coots with all due wonder. Nearby is the tower at Canary Wharf, emblem of the new empire of corporate capitalism. Just around the corner from here you can see its steel and glass rise from the skyline, a light winking from its apex to the four quarters. Directly beneath it is the archaeology of the old empire: the former docks of the East India Company, which commanded its own army to suppress dissent in India. Over the river stands the former Naval College, which once trained officers for the imperial navy. On the outcrop above that is the self-proclaimed centre of the world, grand divider and measurer of time and space: the Greenwich Observatory and its Meridian Line.

The trappings of empire are just a stone's throw from here, but the park also tells a story of progress through popular resistance from when the area was one of the poorest in the country. By the mid-19th century, east London's overflowing middens reeked of squalor and contagion. Some 30,000 people signed a petition for an open green space to relieve disease; the authorities relented and this park was laid out, the first in the capital. Its creation was also one of the original acts in support of what we now call public health, which would soon gather its own social movement to the great advantage of ordinary people over the next century. Besides a place for children to play and learn to swim, the park became a venue for soap-box sermons, political rallies and sit-down debates on the lawns, earning it the nickname The People's Park. In these ways, the park represented a small, people-led victory over the control of an imperial state with its aristocrats and landed gentry. The park's land, which had formed part of a bishop's lavish estate in the 16th Century, now belonged to the people, thanks to the actions of the people. The park's value as a venue for popular resistance movements continued into the 20th century. After Eric Clapton and other musicians jumped onto Enoch Powell's anti-immigration bandwagon in the 1960s and 1970s, 100,000 people flocked here from all over the country for the landmark Rock Against Racism gig. The festival helped to turn the national tide against racist bigotry and showed the potential of music and the arts to draw out the better character of our society.

All this surrounds these oblivious coots in their nest. They do not choose the story they belong to, but we can.

THANKS

Responsibility for the text lies with me, but friends and allies generously gave many hours of their own time to help see this project through, namely Gabriel Carlyle, Owen Everett, Pat Gaffney, Ben Griffin, Sarah Jupe, Haifa Rashed, Emma Sangster, Rachel Taylor, Sunniva Taylor and Christopher Walker. I am particularly grateful to Louisa Wright for her careful editing work and advice and to Emma Sangster for layout and cover design. Darren Cullen, Gus Hales and Steve Pratt allowed me to use their creative work, which belongs to their witness as veterans against war and militarism; I am grateful to them for allowing me to include it in these pages. For their kind financial support to help the project along, I thank Hubert Cassel, Harriet Proudfoot, the Christian Peace Education Fund, and the Lipman-Miliband Trust. Conversations with a number of unnamed veterans have also informed my approach and I greatly appreciate their willingness to share their stories with me.

Bibliography

Aburish, S. K. (2001 (first pub. 2000)). *Saddam Hussein: The Politics of Revenge*. London: Bloomsbury.

Alexander, M. (2013, June 19). *'JSOC and the shadow war on terror'*. Retrieved January 1, 2014, from http://www.nbcnews.com/id/52100170/

Amnesty International. (1991, October 2). *'United Kingdom Conscientious Objection to Military Service – Vic Williams'*. Retrieved May 5, 2014, from http://www.amnesty.org/en/library/asset/EUR45/015/1991/en/80d7738c-ee3a-11dd-99b6-630c5239b672/eur450151991en.pdf

Anon. (2013, May 22). 'Woolwich attacker told me he "wanted to start a war", says woman who confronted knifeman'. *The Telegraph*.

Arango, T. (2011, May 7). 'Face That Screamed War's Pain Looks Back, 6 Hard Years Later' [orig. photo by Chris Hondros, 2005]. *The New York Times*.

Armstrong, S. (2007, February 5). 'Britain's child army'. *The New Statesman*.

Army Recruiting and Training Division. (2013). *'Army Life: Your Guide to the Infantry'*. London: Ministry of Defence.

Asher, M. (2005). *Khartoum: The Ultimate Imperial Adventure*. London: Penguin.

Atherton, S. (2009). 'Domesticating military masculinities: home, performance and the negotiation of identity'. *Social and Cultural Geography, 10*(8), pp. 821–836.

Atkins, C. (2013, October 28). *'British army criticised for recruiting 16-year-olds'* [video].Retrieved May 4, 2014, from http://www.theguardian.com/uk-news/video/2013/oct/28/british-army-young-recruit-video

August, M., Derrow, M., Durham, A., Levy, D. S., Lofaro, L., Spitz, D., et al. (1999, July 12). *'Through A Glass Darkly'*. Retrieved April 16, 2014, from http://content.time.com/time/magazine/article/0,9171,991503,00.html

Balko, R. (2013, August 7). *'Rise of the Warrior Cop'*. Retrieved April 8, 2014, from http://online.wsj.com/news/articles/SB10001424127887323848804578608040780519904

Barrett, F. J. (1996, July). 'The Organizational Construction of Hegemonic Masculinity: The Case of the US Navy'. *Gender, Work and Organization, 3*(3), pp. 129–141.

Barrow, S. (n.d.). *'Alternatives to a "military ethos" for schools'*. Retrieved May 4, 2014, from http://www.ekklesia.co.uk/node/17620

Basham, V. (2011). 'Kids with Guns: Militarization, Masculinities, Moral Panic, and (Dis)Organized Violence'. In J. M. Beier (Ed.), *'The Militarization of Childhood: Thinking Beyond the Global South'* (pp. pp. 175–194). London: Palgrave Macmillan.

BBC. (2011). *'Wootton Bassett: The town that remembers' [TV documentary]*. London: BBC.

BBC Horizon. (1993). *'Richard Feynman: No Ordinary Genius'*. London: BBC.

BBC News. (2007, September 21). *'Gen Sir Richard Dannatt's speech'*. Retrieved May 1, 2014, from http://news.bbc.co.uk/1/hi/uk/7006888.stm

BBC News. (2010, June 20). *'Cost of wars in Iraq and Afghanistan tops £20bn'*. Retrieved April 11, 2014, from http://www.bbc.co.uk/news/10359548

BBC News. (2011, November 9). *'Wiltshire woman's poppy teardrop "violates trademark"'*. Retrieved June 24, 2014, from http://www.bbc.co.uk/news/uk-england-wiltshire-15654558

BBC News. (2012, December 7). *'Military in schools projects get £2m boost'*. Retrieved May 4, 2014, from http://www.bbc.co.uk/news/education-20642796

BBC Panorama. (2007, March 26). *'Soldiers on the run' [TV documentary]*. Retrieved April 9, 2007, from http://news.bbc.co.uk/1/hi/programmes/panorama/6479769.stm

BBC World Service. (2014, January 16). *'Witness: The First Battle of Fallujah'*. Retrieved April 4, 2014, from http://www.bbc.co.uk/programmes/p01pjxg2

Bilmes, L. J. (2013). *'The Financial Legacy of Iraq and Afghanistan: How Wartime Spending Decisions Will Constrain Future National Security Budgets'*. Harvard University.

Blair, T. (2003a, February 15). *'Blair: UN must deal with Iraq'*. Retrieved April 21, 2014, from http://news.bbc.co.uk/1/hi/uk_politics/2765151.stm

Blair, T. (2003b, July 17). *'Blair's Address to a Joint Session of Congress' [Published in New York Times]*. Retrieved April 14, 2014, from http://www.nytimes.com/2003/07/17/international/worldspecial/17WEB-BTEX.html

Blair, T. (2007, January 11). *'Rt Hon Tony Blair MP - Speech'*. Retrieved April 9, 2014, from https://www.rusi.org/events/ref:E45A6104E7E1A8/info:public/infoID:E45A611EFEA3F2/#.U0V64_mY3-V

Bohemia Interactive. (2013, January 2). *'JCOVE Lite'*. Retrieved May 21, 2014, from https://resources.bisimulations.com/w/index.php?title=JCOVE_Lite

Boone, J. (2013, January 22). 'Taliban retaliate after Prince Harry compares fighting to a video game'. *The Guardian*.

Bösl, E. (2013). '"An unbroken man despite losing an arm": Corporeal reconstruction and embodied difference - prosthetics in Western Germany after the Second World War (c. 1945–1960). In K. McSorley (Ed.), *'War and the Body: Militarisation, practice and experience'* (pp. pp. 167–180). Abingdon: Routledge.

British Army. (2009a). *'"Be a hero" for Armed Forces Day' [schools resource]*. London: Ministry of Defence.

British Army. (2009b). *'Armed Forces Day' [schools resource]*. London: Ministry of Defence.

British Army. (2014). *'Camouflage'*. Retrieved May 8, 2014, from British Army: http://www.army.mod.uk/camouflage/

British Army. (n.d. (a)). *'Start Thinking Soldier'*. Retrieved April 20, 2014, from http://www.army.mod.uk/startthinkingsoldier

British Army. (n.d. (b)). *'Cadets'*. Retrieved May 4, 2014, from British Army: https://www.army.mod.uk/structure/32324.aspx

British Legion. (2014). *'Our supporters'*. Retrieved May 28, 2014, from http://www.britishlegion.org.uk/get-involved/poppy-appeal/our-supporters

British Legion. (n.d. (a)). *'The Poppy Ball'*. Retrieved May 28, 2014, from http://www.thepoppyball.org.uk/sponsors.php

British Legion. (n.d. (b)). *'Community Covenants'*. Retrieved May 1, 2014, from http://www.britishlegion.org.uk/news-events/campaigns/community-covenants

Burrell, I. (1998, March 23). '16 cathedrals invest in arms firms'. *The Independent*.

Bush, G. W. (2001, September 16). *'Remarks by the President Upon Arrival'*. Retrieved April 14, 2014, from http://georgewbush-whitehouse.archives.gov/news/releases/2001/09/20010916-2.html

Bush, G. W. (2002, January 29). *'Text of President Bush's 2002 State of the Union Address'*. Retrieved April 14, 2014, from http://www.washingtonpost.com/wp-srv/onpolitics/transcripts/sou012902.htm

Bush, G. W. (2003, May 1). *'President Bush Announces Major Combat Operations in Iraq Have Ended'*. Retrieved April 18, 2014, from http://georgewbush-whitehouse.archives.gov/news/releases/2003/05/20030501-15.html

Bush, G. W. (2008, April 16). *'President Bush Welcomes His Holiness Pope Benedict XVI to White House'*. Retrieved April 14, 2014, from http://georgewbush-whitehouse.archives.gov/news/releases/2008/04/20080416.html

Campaign Against Arms Trade. (2014, February 25). *'Saudi Arabia'*. Retrieved May 28, 2014, from CAAT: http://www.caat.org.uk/resources/countries/saudi-arabia

Campbell, J. (1985, December 19). 'Triumphalism'. *London Review of Books*.

Canovan, M. (2001). 'Sleeping Dogs, Prowling Cats and Soaring Doves: Three Paradoxes in the Political Theory of Nationhood'. *Political Studies, 49*(2), 203-215.

Cantor, J. (1998). 'Children's Attraction to Violent Television Programming'. In J. Goldstein (Ed.), *'Why We Watch: The Attractions of Violent Entertainment'* (pp. pp. 88–115). New York: Oxford University Press.

Career Transition Partnership. (2013). *'Skills and Qualifications'*. Retrieved July 8, 2014, from http://troopstoteachers.ctp.org.uk/skills-qualifications

Carpenter, T. G. (2002, August 2). *'How Washington Funded the Taliban'*. Retrieved May 28, 2014, from http://www.cato.org/publications/commentary/how-washington-funded-taliban

Cathcart, B. (1994). *'Test of Greatness: Britain's Struggle for the Atom Bomb'*. London: John Murray.

Catholic Herald. (1987, February 27). 'Bruce Kent resigns "active clerical ministry"'. *Catholic Herald*.

Child Soldiers International. (2012, July). *'Mind the Gap: Education for minors in the British armed forces'*. London: Child Soldiers International.

Children's Museum, London. (2013). *'War Games' [exhibit]*. London: Victoria & Albert Children's Museum, Bethnal Green.

Church of Scotland. (2011). *'Nuclear Weapons' [leaflet]*. Edinburgh: Church of Scotland.

Churchill, C. (2011, April 17). '"Here at the gates of Faslane, there is no better place to say that it is not courageous of Britain to have these dreadful weapons of mass destruction. It is shameful to have them"'. *The Herald*.

Clark, M. (2013, July 4). *'What do men who've answered the real call of duty think about military games?'*. Retrieved April 20, 2014, from http://www.digitaltrends.com/gaming/what-do-men-whove-answered-the-real-call-of-duty-think-about-military-games

Clement, L. (2010, March). *'The Army: Start Thinking Soldier'*. Retrieved April 20, 2014, from http://cargocollective.com/louisclement/The-Army-Start-Thinking-Soldier

Coghlan, T. (2010, January 10). 'Risk-averse Britain may lose stomach for war, warns minister'. *The Times*.

Cohn, C. (1987). 'Sex and Death in the Rational World of Defense Intellectuals'. *Signs, 12*(4), pp. 687–718.

Coles, J. (2009, February 3). 'Highway for Heroes petition'. *The Sun*.

Collier, M. (2010). 'Hume's Theory of Moral Imagination'. *History of Philosophy Quarterly, 27*(3), pp. 255–273.

Combe, V. (2000, November 21). 'Church drops arms firm from shares portfolio'. *The Telegraph*.

Connelly, M. (2001). *Reaching for the Stars: A New History of Bomber Command in World War II*. London: I B Tauris.

Cook, S. (1982a, October 5). 'Falklands wounded at parade'. *The Guardian*.

Cook, S. (1982b, October 13). 'Thousands cheer task force reliving its Falkland triumph'. *The Guardian*, pp. 1, 3.

Copeland, L. (2011). 'Mediated War: Imaginative Dismbodiment and the Militarization of Childhood'. In J. M. Beier, *The Militarization of Childhood: Thinking Beyond the Global South'* (pp. pp. 133–152). New York: Palgrave Macmillan.

Cronin, B. (2010, September 3). *Comic Book Legends Revealed #276'*. Retrieved January 8, 2014, from http://goodcomics.comicbookresources.com/2010/09/03/comic-book-legends-revealed-276/

Daily Mail [staff writer]. (2011, May 20). 'Glorious Revolution: Chinese army develop first-person shooter game... with U.S. troops as the enemy'. *The Daily Mail*.

Dareini, A. A. (2007, July 16). *Iranian video game rescues nuke scientist'*. Retrieved April 19, 2014, from http://www.nbcnews.com/id/19792794/ns/technology_and_science-games/t/iranian-video-game-rescues-nuke-scientist

Davies, Q., Clark, B., & Sharp, M. (2008). *Report of Inquiry into National Recognition of the Armed Forces'*. London: The Stationery Office.

Dawson, G. (1994). *Soldier Heroes: British adventure, empire, and the imagining of masculinities'*. London: Routledge.

Deans, J. (2003, March 27). 'Blair expresses "horror" at al-Jazeera'. *The Guardian*.

Debord, G. (Director). (1973). *Society of the Spectacle'* [Motion Picture]. France.

Defence Analytical Services and Advice. (2004). *TSP 19 - UK Regular Forces Intake and Outflow by Age Report'*. Retrieved October 27, 2013, from http://www.dasa.mod.uk/index.php/publications/personnel/military/archive/TSP-19-UK-regular-forces-intake-and-outflow-by-age

Defence Analytical Services and Advice. (2010). *TSP 19 - UK Regular Forces Intake and Outflow by Age (2009-10)'*. Retrieved August 23, 2012, from 'TSP 19 - UK Regular Forces Intake and Outflow by Age (2009-10)': http://www.dasa.mod.uk

Defence Analytical Services and Advice. (2011, May 26). *Annual Manning Report (2010-11)' (Table 7)*. Retrieved April 20, 2014, from https://www.gov.uk/government/uploads/system/uploads/attachment_data/file/312539/uk_af_annual_personnel_report_2014.pdf

Defence Analytical Services and Advice. (2012, May 17). *Annual Personnel Report (2011-12)' (Table 7)*. Retrieved April 20, 2014, from https://www.gov.uk/government/uploads/system/uploads/attachment_data/file/280407/1_april_2012.pdf

Department for Education. (2013, November 15). *New funding for military ethos projects'*. Retrieved May 4, 2014, from https://www.gov.uk/government/news/new-funding-for-military-ethos-projects

Dixon, P. (2012). 'Bringing It All Back Home: The Militarisation of Britain and the Iraq and Afghanistan Wars'. In P. Dixon (Ed.), *The British Approach to Counterinsurgency: From Malaya and Northern Ireland to Iraq and Afghanistan'* (pp. 112-146). Basingstoke: Palgrave Macmillan.

Dunn, I. (2012, April 6). 'Christians rally at Faslane for Easter witness prayer vigil'. *Scottish Catholic Observer*.

EA.com. (n.d.). *Medal of Honor Warfighter*. Retrieved May 2, 2014, from http://www.ea.com/uk/medal-of-honor-warfighter

Eisenhart, R. W. (1975). 'You Can't Hack It Little Girl: A Discussion of the Covert Psychological Agenda of Modern Combat Training'. *Journal of Social Issues, 31*(4), pp. 13–23.

Etymology Online. (n.n). *Crusade'*. Retrieved May 6, 2014, from http://www.etymonline.com/index.php?term=crusade

Evans, M. (2014, October 5). 'Injured heroes to join victory parade'. *Daily Express.*

Everett, O. (Ed.). (2013). *'Sowing Seeds: The Militarisation of Youth and How to Counter It'.* London: War Resisters International.

Everett, S. M. (n.d.). *A Conversation: Suzanne Collins.* Retrieved January 29, 2014, from http://www.scholastic.com/thehungergames/media/qanda.pdf

Fear, N.T., Jones, M., Murphy, D., Hull, L., Iversen, A.C., Coker, B. et al. (2010, May). 'What are the consequences of deployment to Iraq and Afghanistan on the mental health of the UK armed forces? A cohort study' ('Supplementary web appendix'). *The Lancet, 375,* pp. 1783–1797.

Federation of American Scientists. (n.d.). *'BGM-109 Tomahawk'.* Retrieved March 23, 2014, from http://www.fas.org/man/dod-101/sys/smart/bgm-109.htm

Fenton, B. (2006, August 16). 'Pardoned: the 306 soldiers shot at dawn for "cowardice"'. *The Telegraph.*

Figaro Digital. (n.d.). *'Case Study: The British Army - Start Thinking Soldier'.* Retrieved April 20, 2014, from http://www.figarodigital.co.uk/case-study/The-British-Army-Start-Thinking-Soldier.aspx

Forces Sauces. (2013). *Home page.* Retrieved May 28, 2014, from http://www.forcessauces.co.uk/

Forrest, A. (2007, September 1). 'Secondary pupils join forces against army recruitment missions in Scots schools'. *The Sunday Herald.*

Free Download Game. (2009). *'Free Download Virtual Battle Space 2 Jcove Lite'.* Retrieved May 21, 2014, from http://freesoftgame.blogspot.co.uk/2011/06/system-requirements-pentium-iv-2.html

Freire, P. (1996 – first pub. 1970). *'Pedagogy of the Oppressed'.* London: Penguin.

Frye, N. (2006). *Anatomy of criticism: four essays.* (R. Denham, Ed.) Toronto: University of Toronto Press.

Gage, W. (2011). *'The Baha Mousa Public Inquiry Report'.* London: The Stationery Office.

Gee, D. (2008). *'Informed Choice? Armed forces recruitment practice in the United Kingdom'.* London: Informed Choice.

Gee, D. (2013). *'The Last Ambush: Aspects of mental health in the British armed forces'.* London: ForcesWatch.

Gee, D., & Goodman, A. (2010). *'Army recruiters visit London's poorest schools most often'.* Retrieved April 23, 2013, from http://www.informedchoice.org.uk/armyvisitstoschools.pdf

Gee, D., & Goodman, A. (2013). *'Young age at Army enlistment is associated with greater war zone risks'.* Retrieved September 3, 2013, from http://www.forceswatch.net/sites/default/files/Young_age_at_army_enlistment_greater_risks%28FINAL%29.pdf

Geen, R. G. (1994). 'Television and Aggression: Recent Developments in Research and Theory'. In Zillmann, D., Bryant, J., & Huston, A.C. (Eds.), *Media, Children and the Family* (pp. pp. 151–162). Hillsdale, NJ: Lawrence Earlbaum Associates.

Gibson, O. (2005, November 19). *'Shopper's eye view of ads that pass us by'.* Retrieved April 4, 2014, from http://www.theguardian.com/media/2005/nov/19/advertising.marketingandpr

Gilbert, M. (1975). *Winston S. Churchill: Volume IV, 1916-1922.* London: Heinemann.

Glenton, J. (2013, May 4). 'Soldier worship blinds Britain to the grim reality of war'. *The Guardian.*

Green, G., Emslie, C., O'Neill, D., Hunt, K., & Walker, S. (2010). 'Exploring the ambiguities of masculinity in accounts of emotional distress in the military among young ex-servicemen'. *Journal of Social Science and Medicine, 71*(8), pp. 1480–1488.

Grossman, D. (2009 (first pub. 1995)). *'On Killing: The Psychological Cost of Learning to Kill in War and Society'*. New York: Back Bay Books.

H M Government. (2010a). *Securing Britain in an Age of Uncertainty: The Strategic Defence and Security Review*. London: The Stationery Office.

H M Government. (2010b). *A Strong Britain in an Age of Uncertainty: The National Security Strategy*. London: The Stationery Office.

Hall, B. (2005, July 19). 'Intelligence report forces Blair on to defensive'. *Financial Times*.

Hallock, D. (1999). *'Bloody Hell: The price soldiers pay'*. Robertsbridge, Sussex: Plough.

Hamilton, A. (1982, October 5). 'Falklands wounded join salute'. *The Times*, p. 2.

Hansard. (2010). HC Deb, 4 October, c1316W.

Hansard. (2011). HC Deb, 16 March, c291.

Hansard. (2013a). HC Deb, 13 May, c99W.

Hansard. (2013b). HC Deb, 18 December, c682W-684W.

Hansard. (2014). HC Deb, 7 April, c90W-c91W.

Hastings, M. (2009, November 6). 'Don't fool yourselves... Afghanistan is an unwinnable war'. *The Daily Mail*.

Herman, J.L. (2001 (first publ. 1992)). *'Trauma and recovery: From domestic abuse to political terror'*. London: Pandora.

Heyward, I.C. (1982). *The Redemption of God: A Theology of Mutual Relation*. Lanham, MD: University Press of America.

Hochschild, A. (2012). *To End All Wars: A story of protest and patriotism in the First World War*. London: Pan Macmillan.

Hockey, J. (1986). *'Squaddies: Portrait of a Subculture'*. Exeter: Exeter University.

'Hollywood and the Pentagon: A Dangerous Liaison' (2003). [Motion Picture]. Canada.

House of Commons Defence Committee. (2008). *'Recruiting and retaining Armed Forces personnel: Fourteenth Report of 2007–08'*. London: The Stationery Office.

Huesmann, L.R., & Eron, L.D. (1986). 'The Development of Aggression in American Children as a Consequence of Television Violence Viewing'. In Huesmann, L.R., & Eron, L.D. (Eds.), *'Television and the Aggressive Child: A Cross-National Comparison'* (pp. 45–80). Hillsdale, NJ: Lawrence Erlbaum.

Hughes, T. (1970). 'Myth and education'. *Children's Literature in Education, 1*(1), pp. 55–70.

International Committee of the Red Cross. (2004). *'Report of the International Committee of the Red Cross (ICRC) on the treatment by the Coalition Forces of Prisoners of War and other protected persons by the Geneva Conventions in Iraq during arrest, internment and interrogation'*. Geneva: ICRC.

International Rescue Committee. (2009, September 10). *'Misleading Army TV ad puts aid workers and recipients at risk, say UK aid agencies'*. Retrieved April 20, 2014, from http://www.rescue-uk.org/irc-uk/misleading-army-tv-ad-puts-aid-workers-and-recipients-risk-say-uk-aid-agencies

Iraq Body Count. (2014, April 18). *'Documented civilian deaths from violence'*. Retrieved April 19, 2014, from https://www.iraqbodycount.org/database/

Iversen, A., Dyson, C., Smith, N., Greenberg, N., Walwyn, R., Unwin, C., et al. (2005). '"Goodbye and good luck": the mental health needs and treatment experiences of British ex-service personnel'. *British Journal of Psychiatry, 186*, pp. 480–486.

Jack Morton. (2010, January 28). *'Start Thinking Soldier: British Army Campaign'*. Retrieved April 20, 2014, from https://www.youtube.com/watch?v=UxxqHwPEwfU

Jenkins, M. (2009). 'Introduction to Society of the Spectacle by Guy Debord'. In Jenkins, M. (Ed.), *'Society of the Spectacle' (trans. Ken Knabb)*. Eastbourne: Soul Bay.

Joyner, J. (2013, July 30). *'Blackhawk helicopters buzz Chicago skies for training exercise'.* Retrieved April 8, 2014, from http://www.myfoxchicago.com/story/22914511/ blackhawk-helicopters-buzz-chicago-skies-for-training-exercise

Klaidman, D. (2012, May 28). 'Drones: The Silent Killers'. *Newsweek.*

Kuma Games. (2006). *'About Kuma Reality Games'.* Retrieved April 19, 2014, from http://www.kumawar.com/about.php

Lamar, J.V. (1986, November 24). *'The Pentagon Goes Hollywood'.* Retrieved April 16, 2014, from http://content.time.com/time/magazine/article/0,9171,962933,00.html

Lévi-Strauss, C. (1987). *Introduction to the Work of Marcel Mauss.* (F. Baker, Trans.) London: Routledge & Kegan Paul.

Linz, D.G., & Donnerstein, E. (1989). 'The Effects of Violent Messages in the Mass Media'. In Bradac, J.J. (Ed.), *'Message Effects in Communication Science'* (pp. 263-293). Newbury Park, CA: Sage.

Longmate, N. (2007 (first pub. 1983)). *'The Bombers: The RAF Offensive against Germany, 1939-1945'.* London: Hutchinson.

Lukowiak, K. (1999). *'A Soldier's Song: True stories from the Falklands' (first publ. 1993)* (2nd ed.). London: Phoenix.

MacManus, D., Dean, K., Al Bakir, M., Iversen, A., Hull, L., Fahy, T., et al. (2012). 'Violent behaviour in UK military personnel returning home after deployment'. *Psychological Medicine, 42,* pp. 1663–1673.

MacManus, D., Dean, K., Jones, M., Rona, R., Greenberg, N., Hull, L., et al. (2013). 'Violent offending by UK military personnel deployed to Iraq and Afghanistan: a data linkage cohort study'. *The Lancet, 381,* pp. 907–917.

Marin, P. (1981, November). 'Living in Moral Pain'. *Psychology Today,* pp. 66–80.

Mascaro, M. P. (Director). (2003). *Hollywood and The Pentagon: A Dangerous Liaison* [Motion Picture].

McCarthy, M. (1982, October 4). 'Banned From the Victory Parade'. *The Daily Mirror,* p. 1.

McGrath, R. (2000). *'Cluster bombs: The military effectiveness and impact on civilians of cluster munitions'.* London: Landmine Action.

McKee, A. (1982). *Dresden 1945: The Devil's Tinderbox.* London: Book Club Associates.

McManus, S., Meltzer, H., Brugha, T., Bebbington, P., & Jenkins, R. (2009). *'Adult psychiatric morbidity in England, 2007: Results of a household survey'.* University of Leicester, The NHS Information Centre.

McVeigh, T., & Townsend, M. (2009, July 26). 'Harry Patch, Britain's last surviving soldier of the Great War, dies at 111'. *The Guardian.*

Mejía, C. (2005, February 24). *'Regaining My Humanity'.* Retrieved May 29, 2014, from http://www.commondreams.org/views05/0224-22.htm

Mercer, Nicholas (Lt. Col.). (2011, October 1). 'Speaking truth to power' [letter to the editor]. *The Tablet,* p. 18.

Messenger, C. (1984). *"Bomber" Harris and the strategic bombing offensive 1939-1945.* London: Arms and Armour Press.

Middlebrook, M. (1987). *'Task Force: The Falklands War, 1982' [revised edition].* London: Penguin.

Ministry of Defence. (2005a). *'Army Career Guide to Infantry Soldier.* London: Army Recruiting Group.

Ministry of Defence. (2005b). *'Strategy for Delivery of MOD Youth Initiatives'.* London: Ministry of Defence.

Ministry of Defence. (2008). *'Start Thinking Soldier: Inter Stage Brief' - obtained via Hansard: HC Deb, 7 April 2014, c90W-91W*. London: Ministry of Defence.

Ministry of Defence. (2011a). *'The Armed Forces Covenant'*. London: Ministry of Defence.

Ministry of Defence. (2011b, October 28). *'Benefits of virtual testing felt on front line'*. Retrieved May 21, 2014, from https://www.gov.uk/government/news/benefits-of-virtual-testing-felt-on-front-line

Ministry of Defence. (2012a). *'Youth Engagement Review: A summary and way forward'*. London: Ministry of Defence.

Ministry of Defence. (2012b, October 18). *'Operations in Iraq: British Casualties'*. Retrieved June 27, 2014, from http://webarchive.nationalarchives.gov.uk/20121026065214/http://www.mod.uk/DefenceInternet/FactSheets/OperationsFactsheets/OperationsInIraqBritishCasualties.htm

Ministry of Defence. (2013). *'Risk: The Implications of Current Attitudes to Risk for the Joint Operational Concept'*. London: Published by *The Guardian*, 26 September 2013.

Ministry of Defence. (2014a, May 21). *'UK Armed Forces Annual Personnel Report (1 April 2014)' (Table 7)*. Retrieved May 22, 2014, from http://www.dasa.mod.uk/index.php/publications/personnel/military/annual-personnel-report

Ministry of Defence. (2014b, March 26). *'Fulfilling the commitments of the armed forces covenant'*. Retrieved May 2, 2014, from https://www.gov.uk/government/policies/fulfilling-the-commitments-of-the-armed-forces-covenant

Ministry of Defence. (2014c). *'Who's supporting Armed Forces Day'*. Retrieved 26 September, 2014, from http://www.armedforcesday.org.uk/supporters/index.aspx

Ministry of Defence. (2014d, April 25). *'Armed Forces Day April 2014 Newsletter'* [email]. London.

Ministry of Defence. (2014e, May 31). *'Afghanistan Casualty and Fatality Tables'*. Retrieved June 27, 2014, from https://www.gov.uk/government/uploads/system/uploads/attachment_data/file/320828/British_casualties_in_Afghanistan_7oct01_to_31_May_14.pdf

Morris, S. (2009, July 18). 'The myth of Heroes' Highway'. *The Guardian*.

Morris, S. (2011, September 1). 'Wootton Bassett marks end of repatriation days'. *The Guardian*.

Movement for the Abolition of War. (2007, Spring). 'Clergy Against Nuclear Arms (CANA) at Faslane in March'. *Abolish War*, p. 6.

Nielsen. (2013, February 21). *'US Moviegoers Can't Get Enough Action'*. Retrieved June 2, 2014, from http://www.nielsen.com/us/en/newswire/2013/u-s-moviegoers-cant-get-enough-action.html

Norton-Taylor, R. (2013, May 30). 'Afghanistan war has cost Britain more than £37bn, new book claims'. *The Guardian*.

Obama, B. (2009). *'President Barack Obama's Inaugural Address'*. Washington DC: The White House.

Orwell, G. (2003 (first pub. 1940)). 'My Country Right or Left'. In G. Orwell, *Shooting an Elephant and other essays* (pp. 149–155). London: Penguin.

Pacull, E. (Director). (2004). *'Operation Hollywood: How the Pentagon Shapes and Censors the Movies'* [Motion Picture]. United States.

Parris, M. (2014, April 5). 'Afghanistan was a crime. Here are the guilty'. *The Times*.

Partington, W. (1982, October 4). 'Disabled heroes banned from the victory parade'. *The Daily Express*, p. 3.

Payne, M. T., & Frank, D. (2012, October 31). *'Marketing Militainment in a Post-bin Laden World'*. Retrieved May 2, 2014, from http://mediacommons.futureofthebook.org/imr/2012/10/31/marketing-militainment-post-bin-laden-world

Peace Pledge Union. (2014). *'PPU Sales: White poppies"*. Retrieved June 24, 2014, from http://www.ppu.org.uk/ppushop/

Peace Pledge Union. (n.d.). *'Conscientious objection in Britain during the Second World War'*. Retrieved June 4, 2014, from http://www.ppu.org.uk/learn/infodocs/cos/st_co_wwtwo.html

Pearce, J. (2008, June 23). 'Arthur Galston, Agent Orange Researcher, Is Dead at 88'. *The New York Times*.

Perlo-Freeman, S., & Solmirano, C. (2014). *'Trends in world military expenditure'*. Stockholm: Stockholm International Peace Research Institute.

Perera, J., & Thomas, A. (1985). '"This horrible natural experiment"'. *New Scientist*, pp. 34-36.

Plastow, J. (2011). *Youth Engagement Review: Final Report*. London: Ministry of Defence.

Power, M. (2013, October 23). *'Confessions of a Drone Warrior'*. Retrieved April 23, 2014, from http://www.gq.com/news-politics/big-issues/201311/drone-uav-pilot-assassination

Prescott, J. F. (1985). *In Flanders Fields: The Story of John McCrae*. Erin, Ontario: Boston Mills Press.

Press Association. (2013, January 21). 'Prince Harry finishes four-month tour of Afghanistan - video'. *The Guardian*.

Publicis. (2012). *'Start Thinking Soldier' [video]*. Retrieved April 20, 2014, from http://vimeo.com/28354791

Q A Research. (2009, March 16). *'Army Recruitment Research'*. Retrieved March 17, 2013, from http://www.qaresearch.co.uk

Queen Elizabeth II. (2013, December 25). *'Christmas Broadcast 2013'*. Retrieved April 28, 2014, from https://www.royal.gov.uk/ImagesandBroadcasts/TheQueensChristmasBroadcasts/ChristmasBroadcasts/ThedQueensChristmasBroadcast2013.aspx

Radhakrishnan, S., & Moore, C. A. (Eds.). (1957). *A Sourcebook in Indian Philosophy*. Princeton, NJ: Princeton University Press.

RAF. (2014). *'Royal Air Force Waddington International Air Show'*. Retrieved July 5, 2014, from Waddington International Airshow: http://www.waddingtonairshow.co.uk/

RAF Museum. (2014). *'Biggles and Chums' [exhibition]*. London.

Rai, M. (2006). *7/7: The London Bombings, Islam and the Iraq War: The London Bombings and the Iraq War*. London: Pluto.

Robinson, D. (2014, May 10). 'Brize bridging the gap between two different worlds'. *Bicester Advertiser*.

Roy, A. (1982, October 5). 'The Falklands wounded will parade'. *Daily Mail*, p. 2.

Royle, T. (1987). *War Report: The war correspondent's view of battle from the Crimea to the Falklands*. London: Grafton.

Rusk, D. (1961, November 24). *'Foreign Relations of the United States, 1961–1963: Volume 1 (Vietnam, 1961, Document 275): "Memorandum from the Secretary of State to the President"'*. Retrieved May 13, 2014, from http://history.state.gov/historicaldocuments/frus1961-63v01/d275

Sandars, N. K. (Ed.). (1971). *Poems of Heaven and Hell from Ancient Mesopotamia*. (N. K. Sandars, Trans.) London: Penguin.

Scarry, E. (1985). *'The Body in Pain: The making and unmaking of the world'*. Oxford: Oxford University Press.

Schulze von Glasser, M. (2013). 'On-screen warfare'. In Everett, O. (Ed.), *Sowing Seeds: The Militarisation of Youth and How to Counter It'* (pp. 49–55). London: War Resisters International.

Scott Tyson, A. (2005, April 19). *'Increased Security In Fallujah Slows Efforts to Rebuild'.* Retrieved May 2, 2014, from http://www.washingtonpost.com/wp-dyn/articles/A64292-2005Apr18.html

Scottish Government. (2012). *'School Meals: 2012'.* Retrieved May 4, 2014, from www.scotland.gov.uk/Resource/0039/00395712.xls

Serie, J. (2014, January 23). 'More than 2,400 dead as Obama's drone campaign marks five years'. *Bureau of Investigative Journalism.*

Simons, G. (1996). *Iraq: From Sumer to Saddam (Second Edition).* London: MacMillan.

Sinclair, B. (2009, December 8). *'America's Army bill: $32.8 million'* [gamespot.com]. Retrieved April 18, 2014, from http://www.gamespot.com/articles/americas-army-bill-328-million/1100-6242635/

Singer, T., Seymour, B., O'Doherty, J., Kaube, H., Dolan, R. J., & Frith, C. D. (2004). 'Empathy for Pain Involves the Affective but Not Sensory Components of Pain'. *Science, 303*(5661), pp. 1157–1162.

Sinor, J. (2003). 'Inscribing Ordinary Trauma in the Diary of a Military Child'. *Biography, 26*(3), pp. 405–427.

Sirota, D. (2011, August 26). *'25 years later, how 'Top Gun' made America love war'.* Retrieved April 15, 2014, from http://www.washingtonpost.com/opinions/25-years-later-remembering-how-top-gun-changed-americas-feelings-about-war/2011/08/15/gIQAU6qJgJ_story.html

Sky News. (2013, November 8). 'Army Urged To Stop Recruitment Of Under-18s'. *Sky News.*

Slater, H. (2010, October 22). *'Helen Slater interview: Supergirl, Smallville, Ruthless People, making music and more' [interviewed by Simon Brew].* Retrieved April 14, 2014, from http://www.denofgeek.com/movies/16528/helen-slater-interview-supergirl-smallville-ruthless-people-making-music-and-more

Snow, C. P. (1961). *Science and Government.* London: Oxford University Press.

SSAFA. (2013). *'Camo Day 28 June 2013: Support Our Forces and Families'.* Retrieved June 4, 2014, from https://www.youtube.com/watch?v=3uQ5XFmfKZg

Stahl, R. (2010). *Militainment, Inc.: War, Media and Popular Culture.* Abingdon: Routledge.

Steam. (2014). *'Counter-Strike'.* Retrieved July 10, 2014, from Steam: http://store.steampowered.com/app/10/

Stirrup, J. (2009, December 3). *'Annual Chief of the Defence Staff Lecture'.* Retrieved April 10, 2014, from https://www.rusi.org/events/past/ref:E4B184DB05C4E3/

Swinford, S., & Farmer, B. (2014, February 14). 'Public school funding for military cadet forces diverted to state sector'. *The Telegraph.*

Taylor, C. (2011, June 9). *'Armed Forces Covenant'.* Retrieved May 1, 2014, from Library of the House of Commons: http://www.parliament.uk/briefing-papers/SN05979.pdf

Taylor, J. (2013). *"Your Country Needs You": The secret history of the propaganda poster.* Glasgow: Saraband.

Telegraph View. (2014, January 16). 'Britain's freedom depends on military strength'. *The Telegraph.*

'Terrorism, Security and Society'. (n.d.). Retrieved from http://www.kcl.ac.uk/prospectus/graduate/print/name/terrorism,-security-and-society/

The Telegraph. (2012, November 5). 'David Cameron defends arms deals with Gulf states'. *The Telegraph.*

The Woodcraft Folk. (2013). *'Campaigns: Military out of schools'*. Retrieved May 6, 2014, from http://www.spanthatworld.com/campaigns/

Travis, A. (2014, January 3). 'Thatcher had secret plan to use army at height of miners' strike'. *The Guardian*.

Turse, N. (2009). *'The Complex: How the Military Invades our Everyday Lives'*. London: Faber and Faber.

US Army [America'sArmy.com]. (n.d.). *'America's Army 3: Frequently Asked Questions'*. Retrieved April 18, 2014, from http://aa3.americasarmy.com/documents/ AA3_Knowledge_Center_FAQ.pdf

US Army [America'sArmy.com]. (2012). *'America's Army 3: Every Detail Counts'*. Retrieved April 20, 2014, from http://aa3.americasarmy.com/

US Department of Defense. (2003, April 11). *'DoD News Briefing - Secretary Rumsfeld and Gen. Myers' [transcript]*. Retrieved April 10, 2014, from http://www.defense.gov/transcripts/transcript.aspx?transcriptid=2367

US military film. (2007, July 12). *No title [titled 'Collateral Murder' by those who published the leaked film]*. Retrieved April 11, 2014, from http://www.collateralmurder.com/

Veterans for Peace UK. (2014, April 18). *'2014 VFP UK Conference – Report'*. Retrieved May 30, 2014, from http://veteransforpeace.org.uk/2014/conference-report/

Veterans for Peace UK. (n.d.). *'Statement of Purpose'*. Retrieved May 30, 2014, from http://veteransforpeace.org.uk/about-us/governing-documents/statement-of-purpose/

Walklate, S., Mythen, G., & McGarry, R. (2011). 'Witnessing Wootton Bassett: An Exploration in Cultural Victimology'. *Crime, Media, Culture, 7*(2), pp. 149–165.

Walsh, J. (1995). 'Vic Williams, conscientious objector and the peace movement'. In J. Walsh (Ed.), *'The Gulf War did not happen: Politics, culture and warfare post-Vietnam'* (pp. 87-100). Aldershot: Arena.

Wells, H. G. (1931 (first pub. 1913)). *Floor Games*. London: Dent and Sons.

Wink, W. (1998). *'The Powers that Be: Theology for a New Millennium'*. New York: Doubleday.

Woodward, R., & Winter, P. (2006, January). 'Gender and the Limits to Diversity in the Contemporary British Army'. *Gender, Work and Organization, 13*(1), pp. 45–67.

Zabelka, G. (1985). *'Blessing the Bombs'*. Retrieved July 7, 2014, from Plough: http://www.plough.com/en/articles/2011/july/blessing-the-bombs

Zillmann, D. (1998). 'The Psychology of the Appeal of Portrayals of Violence'. In J. Goldstein (Ed.), *'Why We Watch: The Attractions of Violent Entertainment'*(pp. pp. 179–211). New York: Oxford University Press.

Žižek, S. (2004, February 27). *'Passion: Regular or Decaf?'*. Retrieved April 24, 2014, from http://inthesetimes.com/article/146/passion_regular_or_decaf

Notes

1. Hochschild, 2012, p. 63; Campbell, 1985.
2. Asher, 2005, pp. 402–403; Campbell, 1985.
3. Personal communication with Royal Mint, 2014.
4. Cited in McKee, 1982, pp. 138, 142.
5. A few bomber crew members spoke out against the raid afterwards. See McKee, 1982.
6. Cited in McKee, 1982, p. 175.
7. See 'Dresden', this volume, for examples.
8. For a discussion, see Gee, 2013; Grossman, 2009.
9. Singer *et al.*, 2004.
10. For a detailed discussion, see Collier, 2010.
11. Scarry, 1985, p. 73.
12. Ibid., p. 12.
13. For example, a TV presenter interviewing me was made to wear a poppy for the camera, against her express and clear wish not to do so.
14. *ITV Daybreak*, 28 October 2013.
15. *BBC News*, 2011.
16. Peace Pledge Union, 2014.
17. British Legion, 2014; British Legion, n.d. (a).
18. Burrell, 1998; Combe, 2000.
19. Luke 12:6; Isaiah, 2:4.
20. Lukowiak, 1999, p. 178.
21. For example, see Churchill, 2011; Church of Scotland, 2011; Dunn, 2012; Sky News, 2013.
22. Cited in Movement for the Abolition of War, 2007.
23. Zabelka, 1985.
24. Ibid.
25. Cited in Everett, 2013.
26. Dawson, 1994, p. 235.
27. Wells, 1913.
28. Children's Museum, 2013.
29. Ibid.
30. Orwell, 2003 (orig. 1940), p. 152.
31. Dawson, 1994, ch. 4.
32. *Lloyds Weekly*, 22 November 1857, p.6 in Dawson, 1994, p. 103.
33. Marshman, 1909, cited in Dawson, 1994, p. 448.
34. BBC World Service, 2014.
35. Ibid.
36. Personal communication, 2008.
37. Stahl, 2010, p. 23.
38. Walsh, 1995, p.95.
39. Stahl, 2010, p. 24.
40. Ibid., p. 23.
41. Žižek, 2004.
42. McGrath, 2000, Table 2, p. 35.

43. Ibid., p. 16.
44. Federation of American Scientists, n.d.
45. McGrath, 2000, p.16.
46. Ibid., p. 36.
47. Guy Debord, in Jenkins, 2009.
48. Guy Debord, letter to Mario Perniola, 1966, cited in Jenkins, 2009, p. 7.
49. Debord, 1973.
50. Gibson, 2005.
51. McVeigh and Townsend, 2009.
52. V&A Museum of Childhood, 2013, opening panel.
53. Defence Analytical Services and Advice, 2004; Ministry of Defence, 2014a.
54. Davies, 2008.
55. Deans, 2003.
56. Arango, 2011.
57. US Department of Defense, 2003. This phrase, more idiomatic in the US than in Britain, refers to a fairy tale in which the character Henny Penny uses the phrase repeatedly to insist that the world is about to end.
58. Ibid., 2003.
59. US military film, 2007 (leaked 2010).
60. Gage, 2011, p. 1.
61. Ministry of Defence, 2014d; Ministry of Defence, 2012b.
62. For detail, see Gee, 2013.
63. Ministry of Defence, 2005a.
64. Hastings, 2009.
65. Bilmes, 2013.
66. Norton-Taylor, 2013; *Hansard*, 2010.
67. Cited in Dixon, 2012, p. 121.
68. Blair, 2007.
69. Stirrup, 2009.
70. Ibid.
71. Morris, 2011.
72. Cited in BBC, 2011.
73. Ibid.
74. Cited in Morris, 2009.
75. Ibid.
76. Coles, 2009.
77. Cited in BBC, 2011.
78. Stuart Griffiths, cited in Walklate *et al.*, 2011.
79. Cited in Morris, 2009.
80. *Hansard*, 2011.
81. Cited in Dixon, 2012, p. 134.
82. Ministry of Defence, 2013.
83. Stahl, 2010, p. 26.
84. Personal communication with Gus Hayles, April 2014. A video of Gus reciting his poem in the cathedral is available online at http://iwvpa.net/halesg
85. Messenger, 1984, p. 210.
86. Aburish, 2001, p. 6; Simons, 1996, p. xvi.
87. Cited in Gilbert, 1975, p. 810.

88. Aburish, 2001, pp. 71, 100.
89. Messenger, 1984, pp. 16, 17.
90. Of his success in Iraq, Arthur Harris wrote: 'The Arab and Kurd now know what real bombing means in casualties and damage. Within forty-five minutes a full-size village can be practically wiped out and a third of its inhabitants killed or injured.' Cited in Simons, 1996, p. 214.
91. McKee, 1982, p. 59.
92. 25 October 1943. Cited in Connelly, 2001, p. 115.
93. Arthur Harris on the plan to bomb Cologne: 'The idea of the operation is so to saturate the ARP [Air Raid Precautions] at the objective as to cause a complete and uncontrollable conflagration throughout the target area. To that end the maximum number of incendiary bombs would comprise the [bombers'] load…' 20 May 1942. Cited in Messenger, 1984, p.74.
94. Messenger, 1984, p, 189.
95. McKee, 1982, pp. 100–101.
96. Ibid., pp. 95–98, 105–6.
97. 25 January 1945. McKee, 1982, p. 101.
98. McKee, 1982, p. 175.
99. Ibid., chapter 9.
100. Longmate, 2007, p. 346.
101. Cited in Snow, 1961, p. 48.
102. Longmate, 2007, p. 374.
103. *The Daily Mail*, 1 June 1992, in Connelly, 2001, p. 138.
104. Bush, 2001.
105. Blair, 2003b.
106. Bush, 2008.
107. Bush, 2002.
108. Ibid.
109. Blair, 2003a.
110. Frye, 2006, p. 174.
111. Ibid., p. 180.
112. Cited in Radhakrishnan and Moore, p. 6.
113. Cited in Sandars, pp. 73–111.
114. Nielsen, 2013.
115. Robinson, 2014.
116. Forces Sauces, 2013.
117. Dawson, 1994, pp. 43–44.
118. Slater, 2010.
119. Q A Research, 2009.
120. Ibid., p. 12.
121. August *et al.*, 1999; Sirota, 2011.
122. Maverick, quoted from bar scene in *Top Gun*.
123. Cited in Stahl, 2010, pp. 67–68. Both these ads can be found on YouTube.
124. Hughes, 1970, p. 68.
125. Zillmann, 1998, p. 210.
126. Geen, 1994, p. 151; Huesmann and Eron, 1986; Linz and Donnerstein, 1989.
127. Huesmann and Eron, 1986.
128. Ibid.
129. Ibid.
130. Ibid.

131. Ibid.
132. See 'Control', this volume, for example sources and detail.
133. Basham, 2011, p. 189.
134. MacManus *et al.*, 2012; MacManus *et al.*, 2013.
135. Wink, 1998, pp. 42–43, 53.
136. Huesmann and Eron, 1986.
137. Personal communication, 2012.
138. Cited in Cronin, 2010.
139. Ibid.
140. Cited in Mascaro, 2003.
141. Lamar, 1986.
142. Cited in Mascaro, 2003.
143. Pacull, 2004; Mascaro, 2003.
144. Pacull, 2004.
145. For example, see Aburish, 2001; Carpenter, 2002.
146. British matériel used by Argentine forces included heavy Canberra bombers and their free-fall bombs, and various naval vessels including their aircraft carrier; US matériel included their tanks, naval assault vessels, the battle cruiser *General Belgrano*, infantry rifles and their ammunition; French matériel included high-speed Etendard bombers and their payload of anti-naval Exocet missiles. Their submarine was German. For more details, see Middlebrook, 1987.
147. For details, see Campaign Against Arms Trade, 2014.
148. Cited in *The Telegraph*, 2012.
149. British Legion, n.d. (a)
150. See Philip Strub's comments on *Platoon* in Mascaro, 2003.
151. Aburish, 2001, p. 159 and Chapter 6.
152. Iraq Body Count, 2014.
153. Ibid.
154. Bush, 2003.
155. Ibid.
156. Blair, 2003b.
157. Ibid.
158. Cited in Everett, n.d.
159. Blair, 2003b.
160. Cited in Press Association, 2013.
161. Boone, 2013.
162. EA.com, n.d.
163. Ibid.
164. Payne and Frank, 2012.
165. Kuma Games, 2006.
166. Dareini, 2007.
167. Ibid.
168. *Daily Mail*, 2011.
169. Ministry of Defence, 2011b.
170. Free Download Game, 2009; Bohemia Interactive, 2013.
171. Ole Reissmann for Der Spiegel Online, cited in Schulze von Glasser, 2013, p. 51.
172. Schulze von Glasser, 2013, pp. 51–52.
173. Schulze Von Glasser, 2013.

174. Q A Research, 2009, p. 13.
175. Steam, 2014.
176. US Army, 2012.
177. Ibid.
178. Figure refers to costs from initial design in 2000 through to 2009. Sinclair, 2009.
179. US Army, n.d.
180. Clark, 2013.
181. Turse, 2009, p. 157–158.
182. Ministry of Defence, 2008.
183. Publicis, 2012.
184. Ibid.
185. Ibid.
186. *Figaro Digital*, n.d.
187. *Hansard*, 2014.
188. Cited in *Figaro Digital*, n.d.
189. Ibid.
190. British Army, n.d. (a)
191. Giles Cattle in Jack Morton, 2010.
192. International Rescue Committee, 2010.
193. Publicis, 2012; Clement, 2010.
194. Clement, 2010.
195. Giles Cattle in Jack Morton, 2010.
196. The drop-out rate among army trainees rose from around a quarter of enlistees in FY 2009–10 to about a third in FY 2010–11, before dropping back to a quarter in FY 2011–12. (Calculated from Hansard, 2013a; Defence Analytical Services and Advice, 2010; 2011; 2012.) The lag between applying to enlist and the end of infantry training is approximately 9–12 months (3–6 months in the application process and 6 months of training (for those over the age of 17½).
197. The campaign officially ran from April to September 2009, but the game was still available to play for some time afterwards. *Hansard*, 2014.
198. Ibid.
199. A dull, truncated version of the game, which omits all the filmed material, can be found at http://www.army.mod.uk/startthinkingsoldier.
200. Wells, 1913, p. 39.
201. Heyward, 1982.
202. Freire, 1996, p. 31
203. H M Government, 2010a, p. 3.
204. H M Government, 2010b, p. 22.
205. Perlo-Freeman and Solmirano, 2014.
206. H M Government, 2010a, pp. 4–6.
207. Ibid.
208. Ibid.
209. Ibid.
210. Ibid.
211. H M Government, 2010a, p. 15.
212. H M Government, 2010b, p. 17.
213. Hall, 2005; Rai, 2006, p. 164; Anon. [*Telegraph*], 2013.
214. Bush, 2001; *Etymology Online*, n.d.

215. *Telegraph View*, 2014.

216. Blair, 2003b.

217. Cited in Cathcart, 1994, p. 25.

218. H M Government, 2010a.

219. Parris, 2014.

220. Alexander, 2013.

221. Hallock, 1999.

222. Personal communication, 2013.

223. Hockey, 1986; Grossman, 2009.

224. Green *et al*, 2010.

225. Personal communication, 2013.

226. Hockey, 1986.

227. Ibid., pp. 27–29.

228. Ibid., pp. 23–24.

229. Ibid., p. 28; Eisenhart, 1975; personal communication with veterans, 2013.

230. Hockey, 1986, p. 34.

231. Eisenhart, 1975; Hockey, 1986; Barrett, 1996; Woodward, 2006; Atherton, 2009.

232. McManus *et al.*, 2009; Fear *et al.*, 2010; see Gee, 2013, p. 21 for detail.

233. See Gee, 2013 for a discussion of the major risk factors for alcohol problems and other mental health-related problems among military personnel.

234. For a detailed discussion on the psychology of killing and comparison with other war stressors, see Grossman, 2009.

235. Armed Forces Act, 2006, Section 8(4a).

236. Marin, 1981.

237. Personal communication, 2013.

238. Mercer, 2011, p. 18; International Committee of the Red Cross, 2004.

239. Mercer, 2011, p. 18.

240. Ibid.

241. This description draws on a number of sources, particularly Power, 2013.

242. Cited in Power, 2013.

243. KIA = 'killed in action'. Cited in Power, 2013.

244. RAF, 2014.

245. Cited in Messenger, 1984, p. 210.

246. Trenchard, who invented the 'area bombing' policy used by Britain in the war, wrote: '…[T]he moral effect of bombing stands undoubtedly to the material effect in a proportion of twenty to one.' He believed that bombing should be used 'above all' to lower the enemy's morale, which was best achieved by killing civilians and disrupting civilian society; bombing war industry was of secondary importance to this objective. Cited in Messenger, 1984, pp. 16, 17. For Bomber Harris' views, see endnote 93.

247. Davies *et al.*, 2008, p. 28.

248. Prime Minister Gordon Brown, in Davies *et al.*, 2008, Foreword.

249. Davies *et al.*, 2008, Appendix 2.

250. Coghlan, 2010.

251. Canovan, 2001, p. 205.

252. Lévi-Strauss uses the term 'floating signifier', coterminous with 'empty signifier'. Lévi-Strauss, 1987, pp. 63–64.

253. Ministry of Defence, 2014b.

254. The Military Covenant is sometimes called the Armed Forces Covenant.

255. Cited in Taylor, 2011.

256. Ministry of Defence, 2011a.

257. Taylor, 2011.

258. Herman, 2001.

259. After a campaign spanning six decades, the soldiers were eventually pardoned. Fenton, 2006.

260. McCarthy, 1982; Partington, 1982; Roy, 1982; Evans, 1982; Hamilton, 1982.

261. Hamilton, 1982.

262. Cited in Roy, 1982.

263. Cited in *BBC News*, 2007.

264. Queen Elizabeth II, 2013.

265. Robinson, 2014.

266. For example, see RAF Museum, 2014, 'Biggles and chums', which is sponsored by the major arms dealer, BAE Systems. Camo Day 2014, which dresses children as soldiers and has them marching up and down, is also being presented as a way for children to learn about the First World War.

267. Ministry of Defence, 2014d.

268. Cited in Ministry of Defence, 2014c.

269. Cited in Armstrong, 2007.

270. Information obtained under the Freedom of Information Act, 26 June 2012, Ref: D/ARTD/01/02/08/01/67906. The same denial has also been made many times elsewhere.

271. British Army, n.d. (b)

272. Ministry of Defence, 2005b.

273. Cited in House of Commons Defence Committee, 2008, Ev 42, Ev 167.

274. Ministry of Defence, 2012a.

275. Cited in Swinford and Farmer, 2014.

276. British Army, 2014.

277. SSAFA, 2013.

278. ForcesWatch, 2014 (forthcoming).

279. Ibid.

280. Scottish Government, 2012.

281. For example, see Gee, 2008.

282. Army Recruiting and Training Division, 2013.

283. Atkins, 2013.

284. See Gee, 2013, p. 58 (Figure 10).

285. For sources and detail, see Gee, 2013, pp. 58–59.

286. See Gee, 2013, pp. 34-35 and p. 54 (Table 7) for sources, detail and discussion.

287. Child Soldiers International, 2012.

288. H M Government, 2010b, p. 22.

289. *Hansard*, 2013b.

290. Career Transition Partnership, 2013.

291. *Hansard*, 2013b.

292. Cited in BBC News, 2012.

293. *Hansard*, 2013b.

294. Dixon, 2012, pp. 112–3.

295. *Hansard*, 2013b.

296. Travis, 2014.

297. Department for Education, 2013.

298. Barrow, n.d.

299. Freire, 1996, p. 33.

300. Hochschild, 2012, p. 188.

301. Peace Pledge Union, n.d.

302. Amnesty International, 1991.

303. Ibid.

304. Adults may leave within the first three months after enlistment (army) or six months (RAF/navy); minors have a right to leave at three months' notice at any point up to their 18th birthday. In all cases, recruits may not leave during the first 28 days of training.

305. Grossman, 2009; Marin, 1981; for more sources and detail, see Gee, 2013.

306. Cited in Grossman, 2009, pp. 3–4.

307. Ibid., p. 1.

308. Atkins, 2013.

309. Cited in *BBC Panorama*, 2007.

310. See Gee and Goodman, 2010.

311. Personal communication, 2013.

312. Minors are no longer sent to war zones, although a small number were sent to Iraq and Afghanistan in error.

313. Personal communication, 2008.

314. Cited in Forrest, 2007.

315. The Woodcraft Folk, 2013.

316. Freire, 1996, pp. 29, 75, 91.

317. Ibid., p. 31

318. Cited in *BBC Horizon*, 1993.

319. Mejía, 2005.

320. Ibid.

321. Ibid.

322. Ibid.

323. Personal communication, 2014.

324. *The View from the Drone; Northern Pakistan (23 January 2009)* 200cm x 200cm, oil and acrylic on canvas.

325. Obama, 2009.

326. Serie, 2014; Klaidman, 2012.

327. Personal communication, 2014.

328. Serie, 2014.

329. Veterans for Peace UK, 2014.

330. Veterans for Peace UK, n.d.

331. Rusk, 1961. The compound used during the Malayan Emergency, sodium trichloroacetate, is distinct from Agent Orange but belongs to the same group of defoliants and anti-crop weapons. Simultaneously, the British in Malaya tested the active ingredients for what would later become known as Agent Orange. They passed the results to their counterparts in the US, who used this information to develop their version of the defoliant weapon. For more detail, see Perera and Thomas, 1985.

332. Personal communication, 2014.